In His Image

"*In His Image* is an invitation to become like the God we worship, to see his characteristics become true of us, the people he has created and redeemed. Jen Wilkin's work provides a solid and accessible overview of a crucial part of Christian theology. Any believer who reads this book will benefit from its truth."

Trevin Wax, Bible and Reference Publisher, LifeWay Christian Resources; author, *This Is Our Time: Everyday Myths in Light of the Gospel*

"I have one big problem with this book: people will assume it's only for women. This couldn't be further from the truth! God has given Jen Wilkin the gift of making big truths easily understandable, which is great news for a person of average intelligence like myself. All who desire to increase their knowledge of and passion for God should read this book. All who desire to grow in holiness and be conformed to the image of God need to add this to their library. I highly recommend it."

Stephen Altrogge, author, *Untamable God*; creator, The Blazing Center

"A. W. Tozer famously said that what we think about God is the most important and most formative thing about us. Jen Wilkin shows us how the best answers to what we should do are found in what we become, and what we become is determined by our view of God. There is no more important subject matter, and few authors are as capable at communicating such deep truth in simple, engaging ways as Jen Wilkin is."

J. D. Greear, Pastor, The Summit Church, Raleigh-Durham, North Carolina; author, *Not God Enough* and *Stop Asking Jesus into Your Heart*

"*In His Image* is packed full of theological insight, pastoral wisdom, real-life application, and plenty of self-deprecation. Along with its predecessor, *None Like Him*, it is essential reading for understanding what God is like and what it looks like for us to live in light of that."

Sam Allberry, Apologist, Ravi Zacharias International Ministries; Editor, The Gospel Coalition; author, *Is God Anti-Gay?* and *Why Bother with Church?*

"This book is for every woman who stresses over her decisions, constantly wondering whether or not she's in God's will. Jen Wilkin graciously turns these questions upside down by encouraging us to know and behold the character of God, allowing that to inform and transform our actions as image bearers. *In His Image* presents a biblical and practical explanation of God's communicable attributes that anyone can grasp, enjoy, and apply!"

Emily Jensen, Cofounder, Risen Motherhood; Cohost, *Risen Motherhood* podcast

"*Who should I be?* This is a question many of us don't explore, at least not that explicitly, and yet the answer to this question is essential to everything about us as Christians. Jen Wilkin helps answer this question in her outstanding book *In His Image*. Wilkin takes us through God's communicable attributes, teaching us how we can reflect our Creator God. Her careful study of God's Word and theology makes *In His Image* a must-read."

Trillia Newbell, author, *God's Very Good Idea*; *Enjoy*; and *United*

In His Image

10 Ways God Calls Us to Reflect His Character

Jen Wilkin

WHEATON, ILLINOIS

Library of Congress Cataloging-in-Publication Data

Names: Wilkin, Jen, 1969– author.
Title: In His image : 10 ways God calls us to reflect his character / Jen Wilkin.
Description: Wheaton : Crossway, 2018. | Includes bibliographical referencesand index. |
Identifiers: LCCN 2017052040 (print) | LCCN 2018011739 (ebook) | ISBN 9781433549885 (pdf) | ISBN 9781433549892 (mobi) | ISBN 9781433549908 (epub) | ISBN 9781433549878 (tp)
Subjects: LCSH: God (Christianity)—Attributes.
Classification: LCC BT130 (ebook) | LCC BT130 .W549 2018 (print) | DDC 231/.4—dc23
LC record available at https://lccn.loc.gov/2017052040

Crossway is a publishing ministry of Good News Publishers.

LSC   29 28 27 26 25 24 23 22 21 20 19
16   15   14   13   12   11   10 9 8 7 6 5 4

In memory of R. C. Sproul,
who taught profound truth in plain speech,
and who dignified everyday disciples as capable theologians.

Contents

Asking the Better Question

If you've ever said, "I just want to know God's will for my life," this book is for you. If you've ever gazed at the trajectory of your life and wondered if you were headed down the right path or off a cliff, keep reading. By the time you finish these pages, I hope you will never have to question what God's will is for you again. Or, at least, not the way you may have asked it in the past.

It's a uniquely Christian musing, this question of God's will. Those who have never called on the name of Jesus Christ are not the least concerned with discovering its answer. It reveals a believer's awareness that, to be a follower of Christ, not every option is open to me: whatever the way forward, it is not wide but narrow. God has a will for my life, and based on my unsuccessful history of trying to follow the way that seems right unto man, I had better do my best to discern what that will is.

But that discernment piece is tricky. When we reflect on what our lives were like apart from Christ, we tend to focus on the poor decisions we made and their ensuing consequences. How we spent our time, our money, and our efforts plays before us like a blooper reel, but instead of making us laugh it forces us to whisper, "Never again." Before we believed, we did what felt right or what seemed rational to our darkened minds. But now we know our feelings deceive us and our self-serving logic betrays us. No worries, though. Now we have a direct line to God. We'll just ask him what we should do.

Without meaning to, we can begin to regard our relationship with God primarily as a means toward better decision-making. We can slip into a conception of God as a cosmic Dear Abby, a benevolent advice columnist who fields our toughest questions about relationships and circumstances. Because we do not trust our judgment, we ask him who we should marry or which job we should take. We ask him where to spend our money or which neighborhood to move into. "What should I do next? Keep me away from the cliff, Lord. Keep me on the narrow path."

These are not terrible kinds of questions to ask God. To some extent, they demonstrate a desire to answer the question "What is God's will for my life?" They show a commendable desire to honor God in our daily doings. But they don't get to the heart of what it means to follow God's will for our lives. If we want our lives to align with God's will, we will need to ask a better question than "What should I do?"

We Christians tend to pool our concern around the decisions we face. If I pick *A* when I should have picked *B*, then all is lost. If I pick *B*, all will be well. But if Scripture teaches us anything, it is this: God is always more concerned with the decision-maker than he is with the decision itself. Take, for example, Simon Peter. When faced with decision *A* (deny Christ) or decision *B* (acknowledge him), Peter failed famously. But it is not his poor decision-making that defines him. Rather, it is the faithfulness of God to restore him. Peter's story serves to remind us that, no matter the quality of our choices, all is never lost.

This makes sense when we pause to consider that no decision

we could ever make could separate us from the love of God in Christ. God can use the outcome of any decision for his glory and for our good. That is reassuring. Peter was faced with two choices—one of which was clearly unwise. But often we must choose between two options that appear either equally wise or equally unwise. Often the answer to the question "What should I do?" could go either way.

Which brings us to the better question. For the believer wanting to know God's will for her life, the first question to pose is not "What should I do?" but "Who should I be?"

Perhaps you've tried to use the Bible to answer the question "What should I do?" Facing a difficult decision, perhaps you've meditated for hours on a psalm or a story in the Gospels, asking God to show you how it speaks to your current dilemma. Perhaps you've known the frustration of hearing silence, or worse, of acting on a hunch or "leading" only to find later that you apparently had not heard the Lord's will. I know that process better than I'd like to admit, and I also know the shame that accompanies it—the sense that I'm tone-deaf to the Holy Spirit, that I'm terrible at discovering God's will.

But God does not hide his will from his children. As an earthly parent, I do not tell my kids, "There is a way to please me. Let's see if you can figure out what it is." If I do not conceal my will from my earthly children, how much more our heavenly Father? His will does not need discovering. It is in plain sight. To see it we need to start asking the question that deals with his primary concern. We need to ask, "Who should I be?"

Of course, the questions "What should I do?" and "Who should I be?" are not unrelated. But the order in which we ask them matters. If we focus on our actions without addressing our hearts, we may end up merely as better behaved lovers of self.

Think about it. What good is it for me to choose the right job if I'm still consumed with selfishness? What good is it for me to choose the right home or spouse if I'm still eaten up with covetousness? What does it profit me to make the right choice if I'm still the wrong person? A lost person can make "good choices." But only a person indwelt by the Holy Spirit can make a good choice for the purpose of glorifying God.

The hope of the gospel in our sanctification is not simply that we would make better choices, but that we would *become better people*. This is the hope that caused John Newton to pen, "I once was lost but now am found, was blind, but now I see." It is what inspires the apostle Paul to speak of believers "being transformed into the same image from one degree of glory to another" (2 Cor. 3:18). The gospel teaches us that the grace that is ours through Christ is, by the work of the Spirit, transforming us increasingly into someone better.

But not just anyone better. The gospel begins transforming us into who we should have been. It *re-images* us. Want to know what it should have been like to be human? Look to the only human who never sinned.

Formed and Marked

Wandering through an antique store fifteen years ago, I came across a small, pleasantly shaped ceramic green vase. Green is my favorite color, so I decided to purchase it for its asking price of ten dollars. Turning it over, I found the name "McCoy" in upraised letters on its base. A little research revealed I had made a good purchase—my little McCoy pottery vase was worth four times what I had paid. But I loved it simply because it brought me pleasure to see it filled with flowers from my garden, perched on my entryway table. Form and function in harmony.

But fifteen years ago, I had four small children living in my home. One fateful day, my little vase found its way onto the tile floor. It shattered, though not completely beyond repair. Sadder than I wanted to admit, I pieced it back together with superglue, but its days of holding water and flowers were officially over. Today, it sits on a bookshelf in my living room. It still says McCoy on the bottom and still holds a form that declares its beauty and purpose, but its ability to do what it was created to do is now limited. And the closer you stand to it, the more evident its cracks. I couldn't get ten dollars for it today if I tried, but I still love it, broken or not.

We are like that cracked vase in some important ways. Think back to that rhythmic retelling of the creation story in Genesis 1. For five days, we hear God say, "Let there be . . ." and whatever he declares is instantly so, and is good. Light and darkness, land, sea, skies, and all manner of plants and animals take their orderly place at his bidding. On the sixth day of creation, the rhythm of the narrative noticeably breaks. "Let there be" becomes "Let us make." The creation account becomes wonderfully personal and pointed. And wonderfully poetic:

God created humankind in his own image,
in the image of God he created them,
male and female he created them. (Gen. 1:27 NET)

God created humankind and stamped us with his mark. He created us to bear his image, to be his representatives in our working and playing and worship. Form and function in harmony. Even after the shattering catastrophe of Genesis 3, we still bear his image, though we no longer work, play, or worship as we were intended. We still hold value to him—every human life. We are cracked vessels, designed to display beauty but leaking at every fissure. But God redeems his image bearers by sending his Son to be the perfect image bearer. Christ is "the radiance of the glory of God and the exact imprint of his nature" (Heb. 1:3). And for every cracked vessel being miraculously restored by grace, he is the answer to the better question, "Who should I be?"

What is God's will for your life? Put simply, that you would be like Christ. "For those whom he foreknew he also predestined to be conformed to the image of his Son, in order that he might be the firstborn among many brothers" (Rom. 8:29). God's will is that the cracks in the image we bear be repaired so that we represent him as we were created to do, so that we grow to look more and more like our brother, Christ, in whom form and function displayed themselves flawlessly. "He is the image of the invisible God, the firstborn of all creation" (Col. 1:15). As such, he serves as both our model and our guide: "For to this you have been called, because Christ also suffered for you, leaving you an example, so that you might follow in his steps" (1 Pet. 2:21). And as the apostle John points out, "Whoever says he abides in him ought to walk in the same way in which he walked" (1 John 2:6).

If we want to look like him, we will walk as he walked.

A Path Narrow and Safe

I once climbed a mesa in New Mexico whose top had been the home of Native Americans for many centuries. Because there was no water source at the top of the mesa, its inhabitants made daily trips down to the valley to carry up the water they needed to survive. The result is a footpath worn into the rock, a continuous channel, five inches deep, that loops its way around the steep cliff face, just wide enough to place one foot in front of the other. It requires great concentration to keep your balance on this narrow path, but there is no question that you are on the safest route of ascent.

This is what it means to follow in the steps of Christ. Whatever the way forward, it is not wide but narrow. Asking the question "Who should I be?" means asking for the first place to set our foot to the narrow path. With every step forward, we increasingly "put on the new self, which is being renewed in knowledge after the image of its creator" (Col. 3:10). Yes, the will of God is the narrow path for those who walk it. But we need not wander aimlessly, as those with no sense of where his will would have us place our next step, in danger of straying off a cliff. We simply walk in the steps of our Savior, Jesus Christ.

So this is a book that intends to, once and for all, answer the question of God's will for our lives. It intends to illuminate the narrow path for those of us who have grown forgetful of its existence or have wondered if it can be found. The narrow path is not hidden. Like the ascent to the top of the mesa, the faithful feet of many saints have worn it deep, their eyes fixed on the founder and perfecter of their faith who walked it before them. It shows itself to those who have learned to ask, "Who should I be?" and to look to the person of Christ for their answer. It shows itself to those whose deepest desire and dearest delight is to be remade—in his image—one carefully placed step at a time.

1

God Most Holy

Repetition is the mother of learning.

Roman proverb

"*Mom, my head is pounding and I have to go to class. I drank a glass of water.*"

"*Mom, I'm feeling so anxious about my exam. Will you pray for me? I drank a glass of water.*"

Two texts, received from two different college-age Wilkins on two different days in the same week. To someone not familiar with our family, these messages from the now-flown baby birds to the mama bird back at the nest are probably part self-explanatory and part weird. But to my kids, they make perfect sense. For their whole lives, a report of any ailment has been answered with the suggestion, "Try drinking a glass of water."

I've been teased by my kids a fair amount for this home remedy advice. They joke that if they were to text me that they have lost a limb, I would advise them to hydrate.

So imagine my glee as I sat watching the evening news, my youngest child seated to my right, and heard a doctor report that the best first step for headaches and other common discomforts is . . . you guessed it. The look on Calvin's face indicated that he had drawn the correct conclusion: there would be no living with me now. Luckily for him, he graduates this year. Perhaps by the time he leaves the nest, I will have received my honorary medical degree from the proper authorities.

"Try drinking a glass of water" is just one of many phrases etched into the psyches of my kids. Parents repeat things. Lots of things. Especially to small children. When we would leave the kids with a sitter, my last words were always, "Be ye kind one to another!" Before they could play at a friend's house, the standard question was, "Is your room clean?" And at bedtime, "Have you brushed your teeth?"

We repeat what we want others to remember. And we learn what we hear repeated.

As my children got older, they didn't wait for the reminder. A request to go to a friend's house would begin with, "Mom, my room is clean and I finished my homework." Because repetition had done its work.

It's no wonder that the repository of the greatest wisdom on earth utilizes this tool with regularity. By paying attention to what the Bible repeats, we gain an understanding of what it most wants us to learn and remember.

Who Is God?

My explicitly stated intention for this book is that we learn to identify God's will for our lives.

Our inclination is to discern God's will by asking, "What should I do?" But God's will concerns itself primarily with who we are, and only secondarily with what we do. By changing the question and asking, "Who should I be?" we see that God's will is not concealed from us in his Word, but is plainly revealed.

The Bible plainly answers the question "Who should I be?" with "Be like Jesus Christ, who perfectly images God in human form." God's will for our lives is that we conform to the image of Christ, whose incarnation shows us humanity perfectly conformed to the image of God. In this book, we will consider how we can demonstrate a resemblance to our Maker. But since the Bible's answer to "Who should I be?" is "Be like the very image of God," we must ask, "Who is God?"

Theologians have mined the Scriptures for centuries to answer this question. Stephen Charnock, Arthur Pink, A. W. Tozer, and R. C. Sproul have all explored the limitless character of God to my great benefit, and to lengths that I am not competent to go.[1] Any systematic theology text lists and explores God's attributes. But I hope in these pages to take the lofty view of God presented elsewhere and ask a further question: "How should the knowledge that God is _____ change the way I live?"

I have elsewhere explored the implications of ten of God's *incommunicable attributes* that could fill that blank, those traits that are true of God alone.[2] Only God is infinite, incomprehensible, self-existent, eternal, immutable, omnipresent, omniscient, omnipotent, and sovereign. When we strive to become like him in any of these traits, we set ourselves up as his rival. Human beings created to *bear the image of God* aspire instead to *become like God*. We reach for those attributes that are only true of God, those suited only to a limitless being. Rather than worship and trust in the omniscience of God, we desire omniscience for ourselves. Rather than celebrate and revere his omnipotence, we seek omnipotence in our own spheres of influence. Rather than rest in the immutability of God, we point to our own calcified sin patterns and declare ourselves unchanging and unchangeable. Like our father Adam and our mother Eve, we long for that which is only intended for God, rejecting our God-given limits and craving the limitlessness we foolishly believe we are capable of wielding and entitled to possess.

To crave an incommunicable attribute is to listen to the Serpent's lure, "You shall be like God." It is the natural inclination of the sinful heart, but as those who have been given a new heart with new desires, we must learn to crave different attributes, those appropriate to a limited being, those that describe the abundant life Jesus came to give to us.

We call these God's *communicable attributes*, those of his traits that can become true of us, as well. God is holy, loving, just, good, merciful, gracious, faithful, truthful, patient, and wise. When we talk about being "conformed to the image of Christ," this is the list we are describing. It is this list I intend to explore, ten attributes that show us how to reflect who God is as Christ did. The more gracious I become, for example, the more I reflect Christ, who perfectly images God.

But where should such a reflection begin? What should be the first thing that comes into my mind when I think about God?[3] Is there even a right answer? I would argue that there is. We just have to lend an ear to the mother of learning—repetition.

First Things First

If it's true that we repeat what is most important, one attribute of God emerges clearly as belonging at the top of the list: holiness. Holiness can be defined as the sum of all moral excellency, "the antithesis of all moral blemish or defilement."[4] It carries the ideas of being set apart, sacred, separate, of possessing utter purity of character.

Following the rule of repetition, the Bible wants our first thought about God to be that he is holy. The word *holy* appears almost seven hundred times in the Bible. Its verb form, *sanctify*, appears an additional two hundred times. Those mentions of *holy* in all its forms are related to things and people and places, but its ties to God himself are striking. No other attribute is joined to the name of God with greater frequency than holiness. Twenty-nine times the Bible mentions his "holy name." He is called the "Holy One of Israel" twenty-five times in the book of Isaiah alone.

God's holiness, his utter purity of character, is what distinguishes him from all other rivals:

Who is like you, O LORD, among the gods?
    Who is like you, majestic in holiness,
    awesome in glorious deeds, doing wonders. (Ex. 15:11)

There is none holy like the LORD:
    for there is none besides you;
    there is no rock like our God. (1 Sam. 2:2)

The gods of Egypt and Canaan, of Greece and Rome, among their other limitations, made no claims of possessing utter purity of character. The chronicles of their exploits read more like a reality TV show than a sacred text, compelling the devout to gaze voyeuristically on their lurid antics. But the God of Israel possesses a holiness so blinding that no one can look on him and live, a moral purity so devastating that not even the sinless angelic beings who inhabit his immediate presence can bear to look upon him, instead shielding their gaze with their wings:

and day and night they never cease to say,

> "Holy, holy, holy, is the Lord God Almighty,
>   who was and is and is to come!" (Rev 4:8; cf.
>   Isa. 6:3)

I am no expert on angelic beings, but it seems likely that the *first thing* that comes to mind when they think about God is revealed in the *one thing* they repeat without ceasing: holy, holy, holy.

Here is a repetition particularly worthy of our attention. The rabbis commonly employed twofold repetition to emphasize a point, and we see Jesus employ the same technique in his own teaching with phrases like "Truly, Truly I say to you" and "Many will say to me 'Lord, Lord.'" R. C. Sproul writes,

> Only once in sacred Scripture is an attribute of God elevated to the third degree. Only once is a characteristic of God mentioned three times in succession. The Bible says that God is holy, holy, holy. Not that He is merely holy, or even holy, holy. He is holy, holy, holy. The Bible never says that God is love, love, love; or mercy, mercy, mercy; or wrath, wrath, wrath; or justice, justice, justice. It does say that he is holy, holy, holy, that the whole earth is full of His glory.[5]

We repeat what we most want remembered, what is most important, and what is most easily forgotten. The people of God can grow forgetful of what the Bible extols as God's highest attribute, choosing instead to emphasize another in its place. Some churches focus on repeating almost exclusively that he is loving. Some repeat almost exclusively that he is just. The first thing that comes to our minds when we think about God can sometimes be more heavily influenced by our background than by the Bible itself. Even though the Bible repeats God's holiness, our churches may avoid doing so. If the utter purity of God makes the angels avert their gaze, preaching holiness may not be a crowd pleaser. Better to go with an emphasis on love so everyone feels welcome, or better to go with an emphasis on justice so everyone behaves.

God deserves our worship for both his love and his justice. But his love and his justice are imbued with and defined by his holiness—he does not merely love; he loves out of utter purity of character. He does not merely act justly; he acts justly out of utter purity of character. If we emphasize any of his attributes above or apart from his holiness, we fashion him after our own imagining or for our own ends. His love becomes love on human terms, rather than a holy love. His justice becomes justice on human terms, rather than a holy justice.

When we apprehend his holiness, we are changed by the revelation. The knowledge of God and the knowledge of self always go hand in hand. We see ourselves differently because we have seen God as he is. And we understand our calling, to reflect God as Christ did, in a new way.

Holy as He Is Holy

I would expect the first thing we should think about God to be incommunicable—something characteristic of only the Almighty—but it's not. Holiness is an attribute of God that we can reflect. Take a minute to marvel at that thought.

Holiness permeates the entire Christian calling. It lies at the very center of the gospel. We are not merely saved *from depravity*; we are saved *to holiness*. Conversion entails consecration.

The Bible presents holiness as both given to us and asked of us. It says, "In Christ, you are made holy. Now be holy."

Hebrews 10:10 assures us that "we have been made holy through the sacrifice of the body of Jesus Christ once for all" (NIV). What a blessed truth! Christ's sacrifice grants us positional holiness before God. We are set apart as his children. Nothing can remove our positional holiness. Yet, the Bible describes not just positional holiness but also practical holiness.

Here again, repetition serves as our teacher. The Old Testament speaks of holiness as an imperative, and it does so repeatedly:

> For I am the LORD your God. Consecrate yourselves therefore, and *be holy, for I am holy.* . . . For I am the LORD who brought you up out of the land of Egypt to be your God. You shall therefore *be holy, for I am holy.* (Lev. 11:44–45)

> Speak to all the congregation of the people of Israel and say to them, *You shall be holy, for I the LORD your God am holy.* (Lev. 19:2)

> Consecrate yourselves, therefore, and *be holy, for I am the LORD your God.* (Lev. 20:7)

> You shall *be holy to me, for I the LORD am holy* and have separated you from the peoples, that you should be mine. (Lev. 20:26)

We might be tempted to dismiss these instructions as just one more weird part of a weird Old Testament book, no longer applying to those under the new covenant. But the New Testament finds these words echoed on the lips of Jesus himself in the Sermon on the Mount. He deconstructs the Old Testament laws on murder, adultery, divorce, oaths, retaliation, and treatment of enemies, pointing to a deeper obedience of not merely outward actions but also inward motives. Herein lies the righteousness that exceeds that of the scribes and the Pharisees. What summary statement does he choose to conclude his point? "You therefore must be perfect, as your heavenly Father is perfect" (Matt. 5:48).

It is a statement so jarring that we may be tempted to think he uses it for its shock value. Surely this is just Jesus using hyperbole. But it doesn't sound like a certain listener seated at his feet on that mountainside took it as such. Some thirty years later, Peter writes to a group of fledgling believers: "As obedient children, do not be conformed to the passions of your former ignorance, but as he who called you is holy, you also be holy in all your conduct, since it is written, 'You shall be holy, for I am holy'" (1 Pet. 1:14–16).

Peter repeats what had been repeated to him. Do not be conformed to who you were. Be re-formed to who you should be. Be holy as God is holy.

If you are still wondering what God's will is for your life, allow the apostle Paul to remove any lingering confusion: "For this is the will of God, your sanctification. . . . For God has not called us for impurity, but in holiness" (1 Thess. 4:3, 7).

Simply put, God's will for your life is that you be holy. That you live a life of set-apartness. That, by the power of the Holy Spirit, you strive for utter purity of character (Heb. 12:14). Every admonition contained in all of Scripture can be reduced to this. Every warning, every law, every encouragement bows to this overarching purpose. Every story of every figure in every corner of every book of the Bible is chanting this call. Be holy, for he is holy.

Chasing Holiness

Because our conversion affects our consecration, those who receive positional holiness will be compelled to pursue practical holiness. As theologian Jerry Bridges notes, "True salvation brings with it a desire to be made holy."[6]

Growing in holiness means growing in our hatred of sin. But reflecting the character of God involves more than just casting off the garment of our old ways. It entails putting on the garment of our new inheritance. Growing in holiness means growing into being loving, just, good, merciful, gracious, faithful, truthful, patient, and wise. It means learning to think, speak, and act like Christ every hour of every day that God grants us to walk this earth as the redeemed.

A few years ago, I visited Detroit in early January to see my brother. I thought I had packed warm clothes, but when the plane touched down to a temperature of -2°F, I quickly learned that no matter what I had packed, I would have been unprepared. This Texan didn't own clothes for subzero temperatures. My brother enjoyed gently teasing me about my accent, my thin jacket, my absent scarf and hat, and my inadequate footwear. Unaccustomed to living with snow, I constantly forgot to remove my shoes upon entering the house.

When my brother moved to Detroit from Texas thirty years ago, no doubt he showed up as ill-prepared and odd-fitting as I had. But over time he learned to put off his old Texas clothes and accent and habits and to put on those that matched his new status as a Michigander. He acclimated to his new environment.

Holiness is like that. It is a process of acclimation, by which we learn to behave like the children of God and not like the children of wrath. The more we clothe ourselves in newness of life, the more incongruous we will feel in our old environments and the more at home we will feel with the redeemed. Our separateness will become increasingly evident to those among whom we once walked. Our conversion will affect consecration, a holiness that we need, certainly, but also a holiness that we want above all else.

For this is the will of God, our sanctification.

Note: At the end of each chapter you will find verses, questions, and a prayer prompt to help you remember and apply what you have read. Consider keeping a journal in which you copy or paraphrase each of the verses for meditation, noting what each adds to your understanding of the attribute covered in the chapter. Then journal your answers to the questions, as well as a prayer of response.

Verses for Meditation

Leviticus 19:2
Job 34:10
Isaiah 47:4
Habakkuk 1:13
Matthew 5:48
Hebrews 12:14

Questions for Reflection

1. How have you regarded God's will for your life primarily as "What to do" versus "Who to be"? Think of a current key decision you are facing. Are your prayer requests limited to specific outcomes? Do your prayers exclude a simple request to be sanctified? How might you change your prayers about that key decision?

2. Describe a time in your life when you experienced an acute awareness of sin. What was the cause of your awareness? What was the result?

3. Think of the holiest person you have ever known. What was his or her motive for right behavior?

4. How should a desire to grow in holiness impact our relationship with God positively? How should it impact our relationships with others positively? Give a specific example of each.

Pray

Write a prayer to God asking him to show you your sin in contrast to his holiness. Ask him to build in you a hatred for all things unholy, so that you can better reflect his true nature. Thank him that you have been made positionally holy in Christ, and are being made practically holy by the power of the Spirit.

2

God Most Loving

The love of God is greater far
Than tongue or pen can ever tell;
It goes beyond the highest star,
And reaches to the lowest hell.

Frederick M. Lehman, 1917

It's hard to talk about the love of God. If ever there were an attribute of God bestraddled with baggage, it's this one.

Part of its baggage is linguistic. For those of us whose native tongue is English, *love* is a term we use generally and indiscriminately. I love my husband. I also love fried foods. Surely there is a better way to capture the nuance between one kind of love and another.

But another part of its baggage is cultural. Our culture loves love. Well, at least, romantic love. It is just before Valentine's Day as I begin this chapter. Predictably, searching for a movie to watch on Friday night, our streaming service helpfully suggested romance movies. Can you guess the top grossing romantic drama of all time? Raking in almost $700 million, it's a little tale about two characters named Jack and Rose, whose four-day love story plays out in the unfortunate venue of a doomed cruise ship. Perhaps you've heard of it.[1]

But the most touching love story I've heard recently is not that of Jack and Rose of the silver screen. It is that of Jack and Lucille Cannon, of Dallas, Texas. In 2016, they celebrated their seventy-fifth wedding anniversary, a story that made the local news. In their nineties, they are bent and grayed, both using walkers to move around the small home they built in 1941 for $3,500 and have lived in ever since. When the reporter asks what it takes to make a marriage last so long, Lucille mentions deep friendship and frames a philosophical response, "You have to give a little . . ." Jack interrupts, grinning wryly. "You have to give a lot—[in comedic falsetto] give a *lot*!" Lucille dissolves into giggles.

The plot line of their seventy-five years is not riveting: they met at church, raised a family, grew old together, and never missed a Sunday of worship. The interview was viewed by a fraction of the millions who have watched *Titanic*, and it won't win a single award.[2] But it is a treasure. Though tempestuous romantic love is what sells movie tickets, the steady, selfless love that endures the test of time is a pearl of greatest price.

Love in Four Words

Of all his attributes, the love of God is perhaps the hardest to conceive apart from the lesser, human versions of love that shape our understanding. Human love, even in its finest moments, can only whisper of the pure and holy love of God. And though we may appreciate love between friends or between family members, we tend to reserve the highest value for romantic love. The wild success of *Titanic* testifies to our culture's worship of romance. To live a life without friends or family may be bearable, but to live a life without a lover? Unthinkable.

Our worship of romance has begun to reshape the way we speak of people or things. It has begun to offer alternatives to the bland uniformity of the verb *love*. We call friendship between men a "bromance." We are "smitten with," "crushing on," "obsessed with," "wrecked by," or have "all the feels for" everything from newborn babies to new ice cream flavors. To say we merely love them is insufficient, since nonromantic forms of love do not connote overpowering emotion.

We have even, at times, invited our worship of romance to invade our worship of God. Take, for example, the familiar lyric, "So I'll let my words be few—Jesus, I am so in love with you." Amazon offers multiple book titles, T-shirts, and inspirational art urging Christians to "fall in love with Jesus," to "abandon yourself to the greatest romance of your life." If Christ is the Bridegroom and the church is his bride, this language may not be wholly out of place. But the Bible portrays our relationship with Christ in terms that are less like the sweeping romance of Jack and Rose and more like the steadfast commitment of Jack and Lucille.

Arguably, the English language needs a few more words for describing love. But not so the language in which the Bible is written. The Greek of Jesus's day, which is also the language of the New Testament, distinguishes four different kinds of love, using a specific word for each. Becoming familiar with them helps us understand how the Bible describes God's love, and can help clear up some of the cultural fog that has settled around our own conceptions of it.

Eros is the word used to describe romantic love.

Philia is the word used to describe brother-sisterly love shared between peers.

Storge is the word used to describe a parent's love for a child.

Agape is the word used to describe the love of God.[3]

How does the Bible use these terms? In its noun or verb form, the word *philia* is used fifty-four times in the New Testament. *Storge* and *eros* do not occur at all. The word *agape* occurs a whopping 259 times.[4]

How Agape Transcends

Whereas our common notion of love is that it is an emotion to be experienced, *agape* is an act of the will, "an intelligent, purposeful attitude of esteem and devotion; a selfless, purposeful, outgoing attitude that desires to do good to the one loved."[5] In other words, *agape* does not merely feel; it acts. Two hundred fifty-nine times the Bible describes a love that acts.

Agape is the word the apostle Paul uses to describe why God sent the Son:

"But God shows his *agape* for us in that while we were still sinners, Christ died for us." (Rom. 5:8)

Agape is the word Jesus uses to instruct his disciples regarding those who hate them:

"But *agape* your enemies, and do good, and lend, expecting nothing in return, and your reward will be great, and you will be sons of the Most High, for he is kind to the ungrateful and the evil." (Luke 6:35)

We are not left to wonder at *agape's* scope or nature. It is *agape* that 1 Corinthians 13:4–8 describes, the familiar passage we read at weddings:

> *Agape* is patient and kind; *agape* does not envy or boast; it is not arrogant or rude. It does not insist on its own way; it is not irritable or resentful; it does not rejoice at wrongdoing, but rejoices with the truth. *Agape* bears all things, believes all things, hopes all things, endures all things.
> *Agape* never ends.

What makes this passage beautiful for a wedding is the way it challenges the couple to transcend mere *eros*, or even *philia*, and to express toward one another the very kind of love that God has expressed toward them—unconditional, selfless, active, sacrificing, unflagging, unending *agape*. More Jack and Lucille, less Jack and Rose.

Clearly, this is a supernatural love, not something any human can practice apart from the power of the Holy Spirit. Because it originates in God and is enabled by God, *agape* is unbound by the limits earthly forms of love face. Earthly love—whether *eros*, *philia*, or *storge*—will always be limited in its capacity for at least three reasons.

First, earthly love is based on need. Lovers need intimacy, friends need companionship, family members need support. But *agape* is offered free of need, extended by a person whose greatest need has been met in Christ and originating in a God who has no needs whatsoever. With earthly love, the greater the need love is asked to meet, the more cautious we are to give it because the stakes for rejection are high. But because *agape* is not bound by need, it can be given freely and lavishly, without any fear that it might be more wisely spent elsewhere.

Second, earthly love covets reciprocity. We offer it on the basis that it will be returned. An earthly love that is not returned withers over time. *Agape*, on the other hand, is given with no requirement that it be returned. Certainly, we give it in the hope that it will bear witness to the *agape* of God toward sinners, but we extend it whether that is the outcome or not. Whereas *eros*, *philia*, and *storge* carry with them the promise of shared emotional connection, *agape* may not. We offer it as a one-way offering, expecting nothing in return.

Lastly, earthly love weighs the worth of its object. We choose whom to love based on some measure of worthiness. We direct our love toward beauty, power, wealth, intelligence, or physical strength. But *agape* fixes itself on those the world would regard as unworthy. It has eyes for the poor, the crippled, the lame, the blind. *Agape* looks beyond what is typically valued as "lovable," and determines to love the unlovable even at great personal cost. It is most purely expressed when we give it to those from whom we have nothing to gain. When we show love to those who can do nothing for us, we reflect the love of God shown to us in Christ.

Agape Is a Requirement for Holiness

Agape is both the way God loves us and the way we are to love each other. We have already seen the Bible answer the question "What is God's will for my life?" with "Be holy as he is holy." To the Jews of Jesus's day, the command to be holy was read as a call to strict obedience to the letter of the law. But Jesus corrected this notion, pointing to the driving principle behind the law: *agape*.

> And one of them, a lawyer, asked him a question to test him. "Teacher, which is the great commandment in the Law?" And he said to him, "You shall love [*agapao*] the Lord your

God with all your heart and with all your soul and with all your mind. This is the great and first commandment. And a second is like it: You shall love [*agapao*] your neighbor as yourself. On these two commandments depend all the Law and the Prophets." (Matt. 22:35–40)

This passage is known as the Great Commandment, the one by which all others are understood. I love the way the King James phrases that last verse: "On these two commandments hang all the law and the prophets." I picture my bedroom closet, with its upper and lower rows for hanging clothes. Recently, a plumbing problem caused the closet to flood. Everything that was hung properly on the two rods was undamaged, but anything on the floor was ruined.

According to Jesus, every call to obey hangs on the foundational command to love God and others. Any righteousness not firmly hung on love is filthiness and rags, just so many sodden garments on the floor of a flooded closet. If I refrain from murder, but do not do so out of love for God and others, I have not practiced true holiness. If I refrain from slander or covetousness, but do not do so out of love for God and others, I still sin. Or, as we hear it said at weddings,

> If I speak in the tongues of men and of angels, but have not love, I am a noisy gong or a clanging cymbal. And if I have prophetic powers, and understand all mysteries and all knowledge, and if I have all faith, so as to remove mountains, but have not love, I am nothing. If I give away all I have, and if I deliver up my body to be burned, but have not love, I gain nothing. (1 Cor. 13:1–3)

If I seek to be holy without *agape*, I add nothing, I am nothing, I gain nothing.

Agape Rightly Ordered

The apostle John declares that "we love because he first loved us" (1 John 4:19). And who do we love? First, we love God. Second, we love others. The Great Commandment is given not to show us how to earn God's favor but to show us the only rational response to the love God has lavished on us.

As with the Ten Commandments, the Great Commandment begins with the vertical relationship and moves to horizontal relationships. Unless we love God with all of our heart, soul, mind, and strength, we will love ourselves and our neighbors inadequately. Right love of God is what enables right love of self and others.

When we devote heart, soul, mind, and strength to loving him, we perceive ourselves rightly—no room for pride or self-exaltation—which prepares us to love our neighbor freely. Rightly perceiving ourselves to be the unworthy recipients of the *agape* of God, we become willing to love our neighbor in spite of himself because God first loved us in spite of ourselves. We do not wait to feel love; rather, we will ourselves to act in love whether we feel it or not. *Agape* transcends our feelings.

When we encounter difficulty loving our neighbor, we often attempt to remedy the problem by trying harder at the task. Yet a deficit in our love of neighbor always points to a deficit in our love of God. We must first focus on loving God rightly. Restoring the vertical relationship is the first step to righting the horizontal relationship. When I hesitate to show *agape* to my husband because he has hurt my feelings or disappointed me, I reveal that I believe *agape* is earned. Reminding myself of God's unconditional, sacrificial love for me, I am stirred to love God more, and I am prompted to extend love to my husband freely, as I have received it freely from God. I love because God first loved me. Right vertical relationship with God remedies horizontal relationship with neighbor.

And what does right vertical relationship look like? It looks like the full deployment of our heart, soul, mind, and strength—the totality of our being—in the active love of God. Whatever we desire, we seek after as unto the Lord. Whatever we will, we purpose as unto the Lord. Whatever we think, we reason as unto the Lord. Whatever we do, we work as unto the Lord.

Who God Loves above All Others

Why does the Great Commandment instruct us to love God first, others second? Because this is the order in which God himself loves. God's love did not begin in Genesis 1:1. It is eternal, existing before creation, having found eternal expression within the Trinity. It required no object outside the Godhead. We love because he first loved us. He loves us, having first and eternally loved himself.

Self-love is not always commendable in humans. While loving ourselves accurately is good, and even necessary for loving our neighbor, the Bible also speaks to the negative category of those who are "lovers of self" (2 Tim. 3:2). We have all known people whom we would label as egotists, those who think of themselves more highly than they should. Egotism is an impossibility for God. He is irreproachably a lover of self, being the only one worthy of total love. For God not to love himself would be irrational. God's worth is infinite, making him alone worthy to receive infinite self-love, as well as the unqualified adoration and veneration of everything in creation. It is impossible for anyone, including God, to love God too much.

But it is possible for us to love the love of God too much. We do this when we emphasize the love of God at the expense of his other attributes. Sin can cause us to love a version of God that is not accurate. This is the basic definition of idolatry, a disordered love. Ironically, one of the most common forms our idolatry takes is the disordered love of the love of God. The overemphasis of God's love is even evident in non-Christians. They may know very little of the Bible, yet many know and are quick to quote the truism that "God is love" (1 John 4:8). The statement "My God is a God of love" often has as its subtext the idea that his love precludes him ever acting in wrath or justice, or in any way that does not fit our human conceptions of love.

But God's love is both holy and infinite, which means that all his actions are loving, even when we cannot perceive them to be so. Not only are all his actions loving, but all he withholds or refrains from doing is also loving. When God acts in Scripture in ways we perceive to be unloving, the problem is not with his actions but with our limited perspective. When we endure hardship or loss, we may be tempted to question whether God loves us. This is why the Bible takes such care to remind us that hardship and loss are to be expected in this life. Hardship and loss are agents of separation, but nothing can separate us from the love of God in Christ. It is high and long, wide and deep, and if we fix our eyes on it, perhaps we may be able to begin to grasp some of that even in this lifetime.

And as we grasp it, we can then press it upon our neighbor.

Love without Bounds

Once we recognize that the love God has bestowed upon us is not merely an emotion but an act of the will, we are forced to reevaluate how we love others. Specifically, we must reevaluate our categories. No longer can we parse our fellow humans into the categories of "lovable" and "unlovable." If love is an act of the will—not motivated by need, not measuring worth, not requiring reciprocity—then there is no such category as "unlovable."

This is what Jesus teaches in the parable of the good Samaritan. When the lawyer seeks to qualify the meaning of the Great Commandment by asking, "And who is my neighbor?" (Luke 10:29), Jesus responds with a story about a man who shows love to the "unlovable." It is, of course, a story about himself—and a story about every one of us who has received rescue at his hands. As the parable is careful to illustrate, it is a costly and unsought rescue, bestowed upon an undeserving recipient.

Love, No Matter the Cost

The costliness of *agape* is evident in the cross. Thus, those who resolve to take up their cross resolve to love as Christ loved, in a costly manner.

When we begin to follow Christ, we resolve to love God *even if it costs us*. And it does cost us—it costs us our pride, our comfort, our self-will, our self-sufficiency. At times, it costs us amicable relationships with family, our expectation of safety, and more. But in laying these aside, we learn the worthiness of the object of our love in a deeper way. We find increasing freedom, and as we mature, we resolve to love God *no matter what it costs us*.

When we begin to follow Christ, we resolve to love our neighbor *even if it costs us*. And it does cost us—it costs us our preferences, our time, our financial resources, our entitlement, our stereotypes. At times, it costs us our popularity, respect, and more. But in laying these aside, we learn the brokenness of the object of our love in a deeper way. We find increasing empathy, and as we mature, we resolve to love our neighbor *no matter what it costs us*.

This is the kind of love that marks believers as distinct from the world. It is the kind of love that renders the story of Jack and Lucille more transfixing than the story of Jack and Rose. What is the will of God for your life? That you love as you have been loved. When faced with a decision, ask yourself: Which choice enables me to grow in *agape* for God and others? And then choose according to his will.

Verses for Meditation
Psalm 86:15
Zephaniah 3:17
John 15:13
Romans 5:8
1 John 4:7–8

Questions for Reflection
1. Why do you think the idea that "God is love" is so popular with the world? How do our human notions of what love is pollute the way we think about this phrase, even as believers?

2. Think of the most loving person you have ever known. How did he or she demonstrate love? Which of the four types of love (*eros*, *philia*, *storge*, or *agape*) was most evident?

3. What person (or kind of person) are you most likely to categorize as "unlovable"? What is it about that person's personality type or behavior that makes him or her unlovable in terms of earthly love? What would it cost you to love that person as you have been loved?

4. How should a desire to grow in *agape* impact our relationship with God positively? How should it impact our relationships with others positively? Give a specific example of each.

Pray

Write a prayer to God asking him to show you where your love for him has been conditional. Ask him to show you who you have wrongly viewed as "unlovable." Ask him to give you clear opportunities to demonstrate costly love for others. Thank him that his love for you is irrevocable and unconditional.

3

God Most Good

Yes, God is good, all nature says,
By God's own hand with speech endued;
And man, in louder notes of praise,
Should sing for joy that God is good.

John Hampton Gurney, 1825

In March of 2017, fourteen-year-old Kalel Langford and his family paid ten dollars for admission to the Crater of Diamonds State Park in Murfreesboro, Arkansas. A mere thirty minutes later, strolling along a riverbank, he bent to pick up a small brown stone that caught his eye. It would turn out to be a 7.44 carat diamond of significant value, his for the keeping according to the state park's finders-keepers policy.[1] To find a diamond in a park known for diamond finds may not be newsworthy. In the history of the park other valuable diamonds have been unearthed. But to find one of such size and value lying in plain sight makes Kalel's story an enviable one.

In fact, Kalel's story is not so different from that of the believer who goes to God's Word in search of treasure of another kind.

The evidence of God's attributes is waiting in Scripture, like so many gems to be unearthed as we read. Though the Bible is an obvious location to search for these treasures, we must excavate all the way to Genesis 18 to find the first explicit mention of God's justice. We must dig to Genesis 24 to find the first explicit mention of God's love. We must patiently mine to Exodus 22 for the first explicit mention of his compassion. But scarcely four verses into its opening chapter, the Bible eagerly places in plain sight for us the brilliant diamond of the goodness of God, no digging required:

> In the beginning, God created the heavens and the earth. The earth was without form and void, and darkness was over the face of the deep. And the Spirit of God was hovering over the face of the waters.
>
> And God said, "Let there be light," and there was light. And God saw that the light was good. (Gen. 1:1–4)

God sees that the light is good, not as an act of recognition, but as a reflection of his own goodness, originating in him and issuing from him. God is the source of all good and is himself wholly good. As the apostle John will say later in the glittering diamond field of the New Testament, "God is light, and in him is no darkness at all" (1 John 1:5). God is infinitely good, free of any shadow.

And the Bible can't wait to tell us this. The Bible's first chapter goes on to methodically reiterate the goodness of God as evidenced in the rest of what he creates. Sea, expanse, land—good. Plants—good. Sun, moon, stars—good. Fish, birds, beasts—good. Humans—good. "And God saw everything that he had made, and behold, it was *very good*" (Gen. 1:31).

Very good, exquisitely rendered from the hand of a very good God.

God is the origin of all good. He is infinitely good, so that even what we see of him in the *very good* of the visible creation, even what we read of him in the very good words of the Scriptures, is a fractional representation of his goodness. Both the creation and the Scriptures are limited mirrors, albeit accurate ones, and our ability to understand what they reflect is also limited. The infinite goodness of God could fill an infinite number of universes and an infinite number of books. Yet, the sliver we see of it is still a bounty, an abundance.

Not only is God infinitely good, but he is immutably good, unchangingly good. His goodness undergoes no increase or decline, nor does it waver. In him there is no darkness at all, nor has there ever been, nor will there ever be. He is good and he does good. There is no better version of him to come, no progress from good to better to best for him. God's goodness is his utter benevolence, the complete absence of malice. God does not, cannot, and need not improve with age. He is as good as he ever has been or will ever be. Perfectly good. Utterly good.

According to Romans 1, God's evident goodness in creation establishes the guilt of any creature who does not acknowledge it. Conversely, according to the psalms, God's evident goodness in creation elicits the gratitude of any creature who does. The psalmist writes no less than five times: "Give thanks to the Lord, for he is good" (Ps. 106:1; 107:1; 118:1, 29; 136:1). God's goodness is reason for our humble worship through thankfulness. It is a diamond in our paths sparkling so plainly only a fool would tread upon it and continue on his way. Yet only the faithful kneel to pick it up, this gem refracting light, free of shadow.

Goodness for All

God's goodness is a light that radiates through all his other attributes. It is the reason his omnipotence (possession of all power), omniscience (possession of all knowledge), and sovereignty (possession of all control) are a comfort instead of a terror. It is the reason we can dare to believe that he is able to work all things together for good as he has said (Rom. 8:28). Right now, there is much that we witness or endure that is clearly not good. But under the sovereign governance of an eternally good God, we can trust that all that is not now good will ultimately be used for our good. Like Joseph we will one day, in this life or the next, look over our hard pasts and acknowledge with him that what our enemies meant for evil God has used for good (Gen. 50:20).

We experience God's goodness in a thousand everyday graces—every one of us, lost or saved, great or small. No, all is not currently good, but much is, if we take time to note it. Have you noticed that creation is not merely functional, but it is beautiful? Our five senses confirm that God has done far more than fashion a utilitarian ecosystem for his creatures. He grants us not only sight, but the perception of color and depth and contrast. He grants us not only the sense of touch, but softness and coarseness, smoothness and roughness, warmth and cold. Our sense of taste knows a thousand flavors, our hearing a thousand tones and melodies and pitches and volumes, our sense of smell a thousand fragrances, aromas, and scents.

God could have created a much duller creation and much duller creatures to fill it, but in his goodness, he formed and filled it with color, cacophony, cornucopia. Anyone who has passed a gardenia bush at dusk has known the redolent goodness of God. Anyone who has halted at a sunrise, stilled to the calling of a bird, wept at a harmony, rolled a raspberry across the tongue, reveled in dew-laden grass underfoot, or marveled at the symmetry of a spider web knows that goodness lies scattered around us, like so many diamonds for the gathering. We are fairly tripping over it at every turn. Even in a fallen world.

Perhaps we might fail to be amazed that the vestiges of a *very good* creation endure, even as it groans in the wake of its shattering. But let us marvel that even in our rebellious state, God's goodness endures toward us in a thousand circumstances. He gives us daily bread, and often more than just that, though we are given to the habit of complaining for what we lack rather than contentment with what we possess. He gives us the joy of family and friends, though we are more prone to rage against him for the hard relationships than to thank him for the sweet ones. He grants us, on the whole, more days of joy than of sorrow, though our darkened hearts are more apt to curse him for the hard times than to bless him for the happy ones. Though he had every right to bar his goodness behind the flaming sword of the cherubim at Eden's eastern exit, instead he allowed his goodness to follow Adam and Eve all the days of their life, even after their expulsion. And so he does for every son of Adam and daughter of Eve to this day.

Think, then, with renewed interest, on the words of the angel to those shepherds keeping watch by night: "Fear not, for behold, I bring you good news of great joy that will be for all the people" (Luke 2:10). Not just any news, mind you, but *good* news. Angels descending into the dark night of the Judean countryside, laden with word of God's goodness: Fear not, for the God who spoke light into the darkness of Genesis 1 is doing so again. Good news. Goodwill. And the light shined in the darkness, and the darkness could not overcome it.

Good news was the perfect descriptor for the angelic heralds to employ, for nowhere is the goodness of God more clearly evidenced than in the sending of the Son. Titus 3:4–5 tells us that "when the goodness and loving kindness of God our Savior appeared, he saved us." James 1:17 tells us that "every good gift and every perfect gift is from above, coming down from the Father of lights, with whom there is no variation or shadow due to change." The good and perfect gift of Christ surpasses every other goodness we can know.

This Father of lights, who sent the Light of Christ into the world, did so to illuminate the hearts of his children, one after another. Christ radiated perfect goodness in perfect obedience to the Father for the sake of the lost. Just as Christ radiates the goodness of God, so now should we. And according to him, that goodness should be evident in our lives.

Good as He Is Good

"Be good."

How many times did I say it as I walked out the door, leaving my kids in the care of another? Spoken in that context, it expressed a parting wish that the little one to whom it is spoken would, at bare minimum, not do anything bad, and at best, be a source of help and joy to the caregiver in charge. When the kids were small, it was hard to find sitters brave enough to take on all four of them. It was harder still to find money to make it worth the sitter's time and still be able to afford dinner out. When I told the kids to be good, I needed them to be. It was code for "Please don't drive off this teenager, whom I really need to have a positive experience." You know the rules. They are for your good. For our sake, please abide by them. Until your parents return, be good.

Jesus spoke a similar word to his disciples on a mountainside:

> You are the light of the world. A city set on a hill cannot
> be hidden. Nor do people light a lamp and put it under a

basket, but on a stand, and it gives light to all in the house. In the same way, let your light shine before others, so that they may *see your good works* and give glory to your Father who is in heaven. (Matt. 5:14–16)

Be good. Others will see it. You'll be a light causing others to glorify the Father of lights.

But what does it mean to be good as his children? As those who are the recipients of the good and perfect gifts of God, goodness toward others means generosity. It means we recognize that God gives us good things not so that they might terminate on us, but so that we might steward them on behalf of others.

The tenth commandment forbids coveting because doing so denies the goodness of God. Jesus speaks against hoarding because doing so denies the goodness of God. Coveting implies a lack in God's present provision and hoarding anticipates a lack in God's good provision in the future. Neither mind-set will translate into generosity. Generosity flourishes only when we do not fear loss.

Possessing the good and perfect gift of Christ, we can count all generosity as affordable loss. God gives good things to us generously, risking no loss in doing so. We, too, should give good things to others generously, recognizing that we, too, risk no loss in doing so. We can be generous with our possessions, our talents, and our time on behalf of others because we see these good gifts as a means to bring glory to their Giver instead of to us.

Generosity is not strictly for those who have material abundance. Because Oseola McCarty recognized this truth, the world is a better place. Born in 1908 in rural Mississippi, she quit school after sixth grade to support her ailing aunt, spending the rest of her life as a washerwoman. She never married, lived quietly in her community, and attended church regularly with a Bible held together with Scotch tape. Throughout the years, the people of Hattiesburg paid her in coins and dollar bills to keep them looking freshly pressed. She found immense dignity in her work, noting that hard work gives life meaning. "I start each day on my knees, saying the Lord's Prayer. Then I get busy about my work."[2]

In 1995, at the age of eighty-six, she contacted the University of Southern Mississippi to let them know she would be donating a portion of her life savings to fund scholarships for African-American students to receive the education she had missed—a sum of $150,000. "More than I could ever use. I know it won't be too many years before I pass on," she said, "and I just figured the money would do them a lot more good than it would me."[3]

Oseola McCarty, child of poverty and child of God, wanted to do good, and generously so. Praise God. Those who know good awaits them in heaven can afford to be generous on earth. They lose nothing in the giving of what has been given to them.

Generosity is the hallmark of those who are determined to be lights in the darkness as children of their heavenly Father. It is the calling card of all who are recipients of the generous good news of salvation through Christ.

Be Good for God's Sake

Be good. Be the person who seeks the welfare of others. Be the person who gives without counting the cost. Be the person who serves joyfully with no expectation of thanks or recognition. Be good employees, good next-door neighbors, good parents, good children, good musicians and public servants and artists and volunteers and caregivers and bankers. If you are, you'll draw attention like a city on a hill at midnight in the desert.

But don't expect that others will necessarily flock to your light in glad acceptance. The somewhat surprising thing about doing good is how often it meets with a negative reaction. Others *may* see your good deeds and give glory to God, but they may not. Cynics call the chronically benevolent "do-gooders." Their exceeding goodness is indeed a light, and to those who love darkness, it's also exceedingly unwelcome. It has a similar effect to that of sunlight hitting the crawly critters exposed under an overturned rock in the garden. Exposing the goodness deficit of others, the do-gooder meets with reviling.

Take, for example, the ultimate do-gooder, Jesus himself.

"He went about doing good. . . . They put him to death by hanging him on a tree" (Acts 10:38–39). Peter's words to the Gentiles about how evil responds to good instruct us. If we are to walk in the light as he is in the light, we will strive to be good and do good, and we should prepare to be treated as he was treated. There is no room among the children of God for any goodness aimed at securing favor with God or others. Only a goodness aimed at expressing our gratitude to a good God will do. Only a goodness seeking to reflect him will suffice. Only a goodness bent on loving our neighbor will store up treasure in heaven. If our neighbor rejects us, so be it. We have done as Christ would have done. If our neighbor accepts us and glorifies God, we rejoice with the angels.

It will not do to "be good for goodness' sake"—we must be good for Goodness's sake—for God's sake, whose goodness we daily enjoy. And we must persist in being good. Paul encourages us that goodness may be wearying, but that it yields a harvest: "And let us not grow weary of doing good, for in due season we will reap, if we do not give up" (Gal. 6:9). The fight for goodness is one that will take time and effort. We may grow weary of our own internal resistance to growing in goodness, or we may grow weary of the resistance of others to our goodness lived out. But steadfastness in doing good will yield fruit in season. As it ripens, it will mark us out increasingly as the sons and daughters of the Father of Lights.

What is the will of God for your life? That you would be good as he is good. That generosity would be your first impulse in the morning and your last thought at night. That you would walk in the light as he is in the light. There is no darkness in him and no room for it in us.

Until the Son returns, be good.

Verses for Meditation

Exodus 33:18–19
Psalm 25:8–9
Psalm 100:5
Nahum 1:7
Romans 8:28
Galatians 6:9–10
James 1:17

Questions for Reflection

1. Which everyday aspect of the goodness of God do you recognize and savor the most? What everyday goodness might you thank him for that you have perhaps overlooked? List several.

2. Describe a time in your life when you were rejected for doing good. What was the result? What did you learn about being a follower of Christ?

3. In what area of your life are you most prone to grow weary of doing good? What relationship or circumstance would benefit most from a renewed determination to be generous with your time, gifts, or possessions?

4. How should a desire to grow in goodness impact our relationship with God positively? How should it impact our relationships with others positively? Give a specific example of each.

Pray

Write a prayer to God thanking him for revealing his goodness to you in your everyday life. Ask him to help you trust his goodness in your current circumstances that are not good. Thank him that the good news of Christ means you are set apart to do good works by the power of the Spirit, which he ordained for you to do. Ask him to shine his goodness through you.

4

God Most Just

In God most holy, just, and true, I have repos'd
    my trust;
Nor will I fear what flesh can do, the offspring of
    the dust.

Isaac Watts, 1707

This is a chapter for those who have been treated unjustly. And it is also a chapter for those who have acted unjustly. Whether you identify more readily with the first category or the second, the perfect justice of God is reason to celebrate.

Yet, it is a topic we often avoid. Many a sermon has been preached on the love of God, many a hymn has been composed on the grace of God, many a devotional has been written on the mercy of God, but rarely is his justice the subject of our worship and reflection. We feel warmth at the mention of his love, gratitude at the mention of his grace, and tenderness at the mention of his mercy, but his justice often evokes unease.

In our conversations with unbelievers, we rarely rush to introduce the justice of God. The typical evangelistic formulas begin with an emphasis on the love of God for this very reason. "God loves you and has a wonderful plan for your life" seems like a more promising start than "God punishes the lawless in his justice."

Yet, the Scriptures find the justice of God a virtue to be extolled, not a blemish to be concealed. And if we give ourselves a moment to remember that we have been justified before the just Judge, we, too, can celebrate the good government and just law of our God.

Good Governor

Good government is hard to find. I know this from watching the news, but I also know it firsthand, having played my part in a bad one. My senior year of high school I was voted secretary of my class, the chief of my weighty responsibilities being to take notes at our class council meetings. My fellow council members and I were the rule-following high achievers of our class, all of us floating through our senior year draped in accolades. With only two weeks remaining before graduation, the local Rotary Club invited us to a lunch in our honor. Dressed in our Sunday best, we left school early, ate hotel chicken, and received plaques thanking us for our selfless service.

It was afterwards that the intoxication of holding high office sort of ran away with us. I have tried to reconstruct the rationale that led us to our downfall, but I can only guess that the free food and the plaques clouded our better judgment. Rather than return to school, we instead spent the afternoon at the class president's house listening to the latest U2 album. What can I say? We enjoyed hanging out together. Which is good, because the entire student council ended up spending our final week of senior year together—in detention, for cutting class. Alas, we were a government that answered to a higher government, the Principal's Office, and justice was served swiftly to those derelict in their governmental duties.

Government is God's idea. He put people in authority to implement a system of rule. The emblem of our earthly judicial system—a blindfolded woman holding scales—personifies justice. Though in human terms, justice is portrayed as blind, the justice of God is wide-eyed and clear-sighted. God knows all actions and thoughts and motives so he wields the scepter of justice with clear vision.

The just governance of God grows in beauty when beheld in the context of his omniscience and omnipresence. The God who is everywhere fully present, the God who holds all knowledge, is infinitely suited to fulfill the role of just Judge. In an earthly courtroom, cases are heard by a judge and jury with limited ability to discern truth from lie. Eyewitnesses report what they saw with limited ability to recall what actually transpired. Bias and corruption may enter into the process. Sometimes witnesses perjure themselves. Sometimes the wrong person is convicted. Sometimes an unfair sentence is levied on a defendant. Justice is not always served in the courts of man.

By contrast, God is a judge who possesses every fact of every case. Though earthly courts labor to reconstruct what really happened, God knows exactly who did what to whom, on what day, in which location, and for what purpose. He knows not only the external facts of the case, but the internal motives of all involved. Not only is he the Judge, he is also the eyewitness who testifies to the facts—perfectly clear-sighted in his recollections. Because he can neither overpunish nor underpunish, his sentences are what justice demands, no more and no less, perfectly fitting the offenses they recompense. No one is wrongly convicted. No one gets away with murder. Justice is always served in the court of God.

God's sentences are also perfect and just. Though humans are given to seeking retribution, God's punishments always fit the crime. He is incapable of overpunishing, and he is incapable of underpunishing. His justice leaves no room for cruelty or vindictiveness. Every expression of his wrath is appropriate to the lawlessness that prompted it.

Just Law

It's impossible to label God's governance as good without considering the basis of his rule. What is the standard that God governs against? As the source of all justice, God holds both the ability and the prerogative to determine what is right and what is wrong. He sets the boundaries for morality. God's instrument of his good government is his perfect law, which tells us what is right and what is wrong.

God's justice is his love of his law on display. In Psalm 119:97, David exclaims, "Oh how I love your law! It is my meditation all the day." The entire psalm of twenty-two stanzas and 176 verses is devoted to extolling the beauty, blessing, and goodness of the law. Ten times he mentions his delight in it, twenty-eight times his desire to keep it. If King David rhapsodized about his love of God's law, how much more does God himself love his law and meditate on it day and night?

When Adam and Eve transgressed these boundaries, they acted unjustly, bringing upon themselves and all their descendants the just condemnation of a holy God. Since Eden, all humanity has rebelled against the good government of the one true

God. Yet, even in a state of rebellion, everyone shows a residual awareness of the requirements of God's good law. From ancient times, humans have sought to placate gods of all shape and form by all manner of sacrifice. We know we are guilty. We know we need provision for our guilt.

Those who do not cast themselves upon the perfect sacrifice of Christ will spend their lives attempting to make atonement by offering their own good works to a God of their own imagining. They will seek to justify themselves by whatever means they can. They will live lives of striving and futility.

But for those in whom the image of God is being restored, the Holy Spirit works in conjunction with our consciences, that we would act justly for the purpose of bringing glory to God. The Holy Spirit prompts us to obey the good law of our good Governor. And what a gift it is to have the indwelling presence of the Spirit to spur us toward righteousness! Instead of futility, we experience fruitfulness.

Thus is the pagan referred to as *lawless*, and sin itself as *lawlessness* (1 John 3:4). Christ is said to have died "to redeem us from all lawlessness" (Titus 2:14). By contrast, the believer is marked by an adoration for God's law, and thereby, an adoration for every expression of his justice on earth as it is in heaven. Paul reminds us that righteousness has no fellowship with lawlessness (Rom. 6:19), thereby designating believers as those who love God's law, as it protects them and others.

Impartial Judge . . . and Father

According to the apostle Peter, God's children should live reverently obedient lives in light of God's justice: "And if you call on him as Father who judges impartially according to each one's deeds, conduct yourselves with fear throughout the time of your exile" (1 Pet. 1:17).

The ideas of both obedience to God and fear of God have fallen out of favor in many Christian circles. Peter reminds his hearers that the God who sent his Son is both a personal, loving Father and an impartial Judge of the hearts of men. Such a God is worthy not only of our adoration but also our reverent fear. It matters that we revere God, for those who forget his gloriousness will soon forget his good law. The Old Testament repeatedly bears witness to this effect in the habitual rebellion of Israel. Like them, we can forget that God is the one who ransomed us from bondage and commence chasing after our own agendas. But those who hold in tension the truths of loving Father and just Judge will "worship the LORD in the splendor of holiness" (Ps. 96:9). They will bring the acceptable sacrifices of a broken and contrite heart, of obedience, and of prayer and worship.

But, by virtue of our humanness, our ability to perceive God's perfect justice and his loving fatherhood is limited. We see only a partial display of God's justice from our narrow perspectives. One lifetime is not always enough time to witness justice served. Often the wicked prosper (Ps. 37:35; Jer. 12:1). Often the innocent go to their graves without seeing vindication for the crimes committed against them. But God's flawless justice requires that he punish all sin. He does not always do so for us to see, on a timeline that neatly resolves like an episode of *Law & Order*. One day we will see his perfect justice on display from Alpha to Omega, but for now we labor to understand what he has done from beginning to end (Eccles. 3:11).

But we can know this: no one gets away with anything. Nothing is hidden from his sight. There is no such thing as a secret sin. "God knows" is a common expression we use to indicate that we have no idea about the why or the what of a circumstance. We often speak it in frustration, but for the believer, that phrase acknowledges a basic fact that should elicit reassurance. God sees and he knows. And in his justice, he acts. He will by no means clear the guilty (Nah. 1:3). How comforting to know that no injustice we may suffer goes unseen or unrepaid.

How comforting, also, as those whose guilt is manifestly established, to discover that the just Judge we must stand before is also the one we call on as our good Father! Imagine being placed on trial for a crime you committed in broad daylight, only to enter the courtroom and discover your dearly loved, infinitely loving, good, and compassionate father seated on the bench. Imagine also, as you stand to plead guilty, your brother Christ Jesus rising to intercede for you. His testimony stands: he has borne your guilt for having rebelled against God's good government. He has borne the government upon his shoulders, in the form of a wooden cross.

Just Discipline

Is justice, then, something the believer never experiences from God? Because of Christ, our Father and Judge does not look upon us with wrath, but he still parents us with justice. We call this his discipline. He gives us laws that are for our good and for our safety, and when we transgress them, he allows us to repent and learn from our mistakes, though often with consequences. And though he disciplines in love, we may not immediately perceive it as loving. This is why the author of Hebrews takes care to remind us that God disciplines those he loves (Heb. 12:6). The prophet Jeremiah recognized the role of just discipline for the child of God: "Discipline me, LORD, but with justice—not in Your anger, or You will reduce me to nothing" (Jer. 10:24 CSB).

God's discipline is his justice without wrath, for the purpose of training us in godliness.

When my kids were small, Mother's Day meant that special projects would be coming home from school. When Calvin was in kindergarten, his teacher sent home a question and answer sheet Calvin had completed about me. He completed the sentence "My mother loves _____" with "naps and Oreos." Guilty as charged. He completed the sentence "I know my mother loves me because _____" with an endearing list of things I did for him. "She makes me dinner. She gives me hugs. She helps me brush my teeth."

In all the years I received such sheets from my small kids, not one of them answered that they knew I loved them because I enforced a seven o'clock bedtime or because I limited sweets or because I sent them to time-out for arguing. Though these were absolutely expressions of my love, it was not until the kids were older that they learned to see them as such. This is the way God's justice functions in the life of the believer. Because of Christ, we receive training from God's law as those who can no longer be condemned by it. We may be slow to recognize it as an expression of his love, but it gives us good government. It teaches us to walk as children of the light, to walk as Christ walked.

Just Wrath

If it is hard to recognize discipline as compatible with a loving God, it is even harder to recognize wrath as so. This aspect of his justice can challenge the faith of those who cling to the Scriptures as inerrant, and it can motivate those who reject or diminish the biblical witness to say, "My God is a God of love, not wrath." I admit that, while my reading of Scripture grants me intellectual assent to the necessity and rightness of God's wrath against sin, my emotional response is more that of a child not grown to maturity, still fighting for a clear perspective.

While I can identify with the desire to edit God's wrath from the Bible, or to contain it to the Old Testament, to do so would compromise his holiness and my posture before it. There is no way to reach genuine repentance without striving to grasp the justice of God's wrath. As long as I view his wrath as excessive or cruel, I labor under a limited understanding of the danger and depravity of sin. And I labor under a limited understanding of Calvary.

The story of the fate of Sodom and Gomorrah instructs me here. When God tells Abraham his plan to destroy these two cities situated on the plain of Shinar, Abraham is moved to intercede that the righteous be spared. God agrees to spare the city if there are ten righteous people within its walls. What God knows and Abraham does not is that there are not ten. He will spare only Lot's family, and he will do so not as an act of justice but of mercy.

I imagine Abraham waiting and wondering after his angelic visitors go down to Sodom. As he waits at a distance, the narrative zooms in to describe a typical day in the life of Sodom, and it is stomach-turning. Sensuality, violence, and wickedness splatter the text. The reader witnesses all of it, but Abraham witnesses none of it. I imagine his shock when he learns of the fate of those for whom he interceded:

> And Abraham went early in the morning to the place where he had stood before the LORD. And he looked down toward Sodom and Gomorrah and toward all the land of the valley, and he looked and, behold, the smoke of the land went up like the smoke of a furnace. (Gen. 19:27–28)

As Abraham gazes over the smoking ruins of those two cities, he beholds a gospel truth: in his justice, God punishes sin. A greater intercession was needed than any Abraham could offer. He does not witness cruelty, for God cannot overpunish. That would render him unjust. No, Abraham witnesses a punishment that fits the crime.

I do not know how many people were living in the neighboring cities of Sodom and Gomorrah at the time of their destruction, but I suspect it was far fewer than live in my own home of Dallas/Fort Worth. Whatever the number of inhabitants, they represented a minuscule number of human lives in the scope of all the unrighteous who have lived from Adam until now. This is a sobering thought: what happened on the plain of Shinar that bleak day when fire rained down from the heavens was what perfect justice looks like for the sins of a few.

But the cross is where Christ suffered for the sins of many. None is righteous, no, not one (Rom. 3:10). The fate of Sodom is the fate we all deserve. At the cross, God's towering justice for the many, for me, white-hot and sulfurous, holy, equitable to the crimes it repaid, rained down from heaven on the only just human ever to walk the earth. Willingly, the just suffered for the unjust, that he might bring us to God.

This is why the Bible reminds us that if we confess our sins, God is not only faithful to forgive our sins, but also just. Because Christ was punished in our place, God would be unjust to punish us for a sin that has already received its recompense. How precious, then, does the spilled blood and broken body of Christ become in our estimation? How quickly, then, ought we to confess? The need for excuses, for self-justification, is removed. We are justified before God in Christ.

Seeking to Justify Ourselves

If we grow forgetful that we are justified in Christ, our relationship with God and with others will feel the effects. We will begin to slip into patterns of denying or minimizing our sins, rather than acknowledging and confessing them. We will begin to keep score. We will become acutely aware of the offenses of others against us, and our anger will be easily stirred when they are committed.

Furthermore, we will become blithely unaware of our offenses against others, and our anger will be easily stirred when they are brought to our attention. We will smooth things over with an apology, secretly believing that we did nothing wrong in the first place. Or, if our offense is valid, we will present extenuating circumstances or lengthy explanations as to why we were justified in our actions. The self-justifier can be easily identified. He will be slow to listen, quick to speak, and quick to become angry—the very inverse of what James commands (James 1:19).

Because our sense of justice is based on a partial and biased view of the facts of any given case, we will keep score in a manner that always proclaims us in the right. As our own judge and jury, we will perceive the evidence to point toward our acquittal and our neighbor's condemnation. Like the Pharisee in Jesus's parable, we will congratulate ourselves that we are "not like other men" (Luke 18:11).

All this scorekeeping diverts our energies from living at peace with one another and seeking to serve. And it is pointless. We have no need to self-justify. We need only confess our sins. Self-justification reveals a lack of understanding of the forgiveness we received through the cross. The cross of Christ means that the score is settled.

The life of the believer who loves the justice of God will be marked not by scorekeeping, but by reverent obedience. It will be marked by a love of the moral law that reshapes our desires to reflect those of our heavenly Father. It will be marked by humble submission to where our good Governor sets the limits of what is right. The immediate effect of apprehending God's justice will be an inward-facing desire to obey. The long-term effect will be an outward-facing desire to do justice for others.

Just as He Is Just

What is the will of God for your life? Hear the words of the prophet Micah:

> . . . and what does the LORD require of you
> but to do justice, and to love kindness,
>   and to walk humbly with your God? (Mic. 6:8)

God's will is that we do justice. When we cease self-justifying, we begin to have eyes for the needs of our neighbors with ever-increasing clarity. We turn our energies toward securing justice for the weak and the oppressed. God refers to himself as a "father of the fatherless and protector of widows" (Ps. 68:4–5). As his children, we ought to carry this family identity into the spheres of influence he gives us. Those of us who have any form of advantage must seek to use it to benefit our neighbors. Those of us who have more than our daily bread each day must have open eyes and open hands for those who are still awaiting theirs.

In ancient times, the widow and orphan were those most likely to suffer exploitation or to be forgotten by their communities. They lacked social or economic power; they had no voice and no advocate. The exploited and forgotten are all around us today, just as they were then. The Bible speaks of a wideness in God's justice, repeatedly calling his people to seek it for the marginalized and overlooked. If we miss this, our sense of justice may extend only as widely as the eaves of our own homes.

Our communities and churches are filled with modern-day

widows and orphans, sojourners, and indigents. We act justly when we intercede on their behalf, ensuring that they are treated as humans created in the image of God. We should be the first to feed the hungry, clothe the naked, welcome the stranger, visit the sick. We should secure justice for the oppressed, because to do so is to look like God. To do so is as though we have done so for Christ himself (Matt. 25:35–40).

God's good government ensures that justice will ultimately prevail in all things. It answers to no higher government, and it suffers no corruption. Until the day when all accounts are settled, we labor as his servants to live obediently and to seek justice for those who do not have it. What is the will of God for your life? That you be just as he is just, delighting in his law, extolling his good government, doing justice daily as children of your heavenly Father.

Verses for Meditation

Deuteronomy 10:17–19
Deuteronomy 32:3–4
Psalm 9:7–8
Psalm 37:27–29
Psalm 82:1–4
Psalm 89:14
Luke 11:42

Questions for Reflection

1. How have you known God's law to provide good government in your life? Give an example from your experience. How has God's law proven itself to be a worthy subject of constant meditation and love?

2. Describe a time in your life when you experienced the loving discipline of God. What was the result?

3. What forms of self-justification and keeping score are you most prone to? What underlying areas of unrepentance do they reveal?

4. Who needs you to do justice for them? List several specific people or groups in your community and brainstorm specific actions you can take this week to extend help to them.

Pray

Write a prayer to God praising him for his good government. Thank him for his law, which preserves you from sin. Confess any self-justification you have committed this week. Ask him to build in you a hatred for human acts of injustice, so that you can eagerly serve those who suffer from them. Thank him that you have been justified that you might act justly.

5

God Most Merciful

Depth of mercy! Can there be
Mercy still reserved for me?

Charles Wesley, 1740

My two daughters were born a scant fifteen months apart. Because of their closeness in age, they went through school sharing the same friends, playing on the same sports teams, singing in the same choir, and serving in the same ministry at church. Consequently, they are almost always spoken of in the same breath. Friends ask, "How are Mary Kate and Claire doing?" They do share much in common, and they make a happy pair. But they are also unique individuals, each with a distinct and delightful personality, each possessing her own version of internal and external loveliness, each adding a unique contribution to our family and to the world. Anyone who knows them recognizes this, and it is merely a circumstance of proximity of age that finds their names so often mentioned together.

A similar blurring of distinction often happens with two attributes of God so closely associated in our minds that they could be thought of as sisters: mercy and grace. They frequently occur next to each other in the same verse. They appear as a pair in our hymns and worship choruses. They are, without a doubt, closely related. But just as my daughters are both happily similar and delightfully distinct, so are the sister attributes of mercy and grace worthy of both shared and individual adoration.

So, we will take them one sister at a time, one chapter at a time. But before we divide them, we must consider them together. To do so, we must also include the necessary context of God's justice. Justice, mercy, and grace coexist in the character of God. When God gives Moses the Ten Commandments, he celebrates all three characteristics in his self-description: "The Lord, the Lord, a God merciful and gracious . . . forgiving iniquity and transgression and sin, but who will by no means clear the guilty" (Ex. 34:6–7).

We have already considered the justice of God, but for the purpose of comparison, let us distill justice, mercy, and grace down to three classic and simple definitions that help us understand how they relate to one another.

- **Justice** is getting what we deserve.
- **Mercy** is not getting what we deserve.
- **Grace** is getting what we do not deserve.

Clearly, knowing "what we deserve" is the first step to apprehending the distinctions between these three attributes. Our discussion of the perfect justice of God reminded us that, because we have transgressed his holy law, we all deserve death. But the mere fact that you are reading this book should tell you that justice has not been served. At least, not at your expense. If it had, you'd be dead, and so would this book's author. There would be no book to read, nor any other book to read, nor anyone living to either read books or write books, as "all have sinned and fall short of the glory of God" (Rom. 3:23).

The fact that you are currently inhaling and exhaling at this very moment means that you are a recipient of mercy. Though he had every right to demand your life, God has granted you days, months, and years. In this, you and every other human have received mercy in being spared immediate death and grace in having been given length of days. You have been granted a reprieve from physical death. And if, as seems likely, you are reading this book because you are a believer in Christ, you have received not only mercy but also the gift of eternal life—the greatest grace of all. But more on grace when we get to her chapter. First, we will give her sister, mercy, her due.

Mercy Abounds

God's mercy is his active compassion toward his creation. It is his response to suffering and guilt, both products of the fall. How far does it extend? "The LORD is good to all, and his mercy is over all that he has made" (Ps. 145:9). God is infinitely merciful, but he exercises his mercy as he chooses, according to his sovereign will. He chooses upon whom he will have mercy (Rom. 9:15). He is obligated to show mercy to none, but we find him throughout the Bible demonstrating mercy toward sinner and saint alike. The psalmists can scarcely stop talking about the mercy of God. Though many conceive of the God of the Old Testament as a God of towering justice, absent of mercy, the Old Testament mentions his mercy more than four times as often as the New.[1]

But the New Testament teaches us that in Christ, we see the mercy of God demonstrated in all its lavishness: "But God, being rich in mercy, because of the great love with which he loved us, even when we were dead in our trespasses, made us alive together with Christ" (Eph. 2:4–5). Paul opens his second letter to the Corinthians with a celebration of God as "the God and Father of our Lord Jesus Christ, the Father of mercies and God of all comfort" (2 Cor. 1:3). Peter exclaims, "Blessed be the God and Father of our Lord Jesus Christ! According to his great mercy, he has caused us to be born again to a living hope through the resurrection of Jesus Christ from the dead" (1 Pet. 1:3).

God the Father sends the Son in accordance with his great mercy. God acts in compassion toward sinners, the Son takes on flesh, and mercy acquires a name.

Understanding the mercy of God in Christ can help us untangle an important verse we often pass by too quickly. It's one I memorized as a child, but never slowed down to examine as I should: "If we confess our sins, he is faithful and just to forgive us our sins and to cleanse us from all unrighteousness" (1 John 1:9). Faithful and . . . just? Seeing God as faithful to forgive confessed sins seems intuitive, but it's that reference to justice that confounded me when I slowed down to examine it. How can God's forgiveness of our sins be just? Shouldn't it say "faithful and merciful" not "faithful and just"? It took another failure to help me slow down and understand how this verse could be true.

Justice, Mercy, and Minivans

My husband, Jeff, is an excellent driver. He has never had an accident, excepting two incidents in high school which hardly bear mentioning—one in which an unexpected cow sustained minor injuries, and one in which a drive-through car wash suffered a catastrophic failure during Jeff's wash cycle. So, to clarify, Jeff is an excellent driver who, though twice the victim of circumstances beyond his control, has an otherwise accident-free driving record.

I am not a bad driver. The only two-vehicle accident I have ever been involved in (okay, that I have ever caused) happened in the church parking lot. I backed rather forcefully into a truck that was behind me, doing significant damage to its fender and grill. The story is more telling when you understand that, in a lot of over four hundred spaces, I hit the only other car parked in it at the time.

I am not a bad driver, but I have received the occasional ticket. Several years ago, I was driving across town to get to a speaking engagement during Friday rush hour traffic. Having waited three cycles to make a left turn at a busy intersection, I accelerated through a yellow light and continued on my way. A couple of weeks later a ticket came in the mail with photo evidence of my depravity. I had run the red light. Justice dictated that it would take two hundred dollars to clear my good name. Or so I thought.

Let's just say we didn't have an extra two hundred dollars lying around, and my embarrassment over the whole thing caused me to stall on paying the ticket. Jeff noticed that the deadline to pay was upon me and gave me a gentle reminder. I was leaving town, and he generously agreed to get online and handle the payment. That's when he discovered that it was not, in fact, my good name that was at stake, but his. Because the car I was driving was registered to him, my ticket had been put on his driving record—his excellent driving record. His response? "It's taken care of."

Mercy. He paid my ticket without grumbling, and my guilt was assigned to his record. In the eyes of the great state of Texas, the demands of justice had been met, albeit by another. I did not receive what I deserved, but Jeff did in my place.

This is why it makes sense that God is both faithful and just to forgive us our sin: because Christ received justice at the cross, we receive mercy. Having executed justice on Christ in our stead, God would be unjust to now withhold from us forgiveness for our sin. Mercy and justice both take their place in the narrative of our salvation.

Mercy over Judgment

One of the hardest parts of writing or teaching is to find and tell stories that will illustrate the key points of what I want to communicate. I prefer personal stories that really happened (like the previous one), but there's always the risk of overexposing a friend or family member in the retelling, so they have to be handled with care. Fortuitously, in the case of a discussion on mercy, the perfect story has already been crafted. Because its characters are fictional and it never really happened, surely it risks offending no one. I borrow it here with the author's permission.

It is the story of the most respected man in town and the most hated, both of whom make their way to the local place of worship heavy-laden in their own different ways. The first man stands and prays aloud, thanking God that he is not like other men. He is, by his own report, the very model of righteousness, and nothing like that scoundrel who has crept in behind him, clinging to the wall just inside the entrance. No doubt everyone within hearing would have agreed with his self-assessment.

But then the scoundrel, standing at a distance, opens his mouth to speak. The presumption of it defies belief. On what basis does he dare to offer his prayer in this place? He utters but one simple statement: "God, have mercy on me, a sinner" (Luke 18:13 NIV).

The insufficiency of it. The brevity and the generality of it, the acrid fumes of desperation swirling around this blurted statement. Go back to where you came from. You have no business here.

Yet, the author of our story pronounces a different verdict than what we might expect: "I tell you, this man went down to his house justified, rather than the other. For everyone who exalts himself will be humbled, but the one who humbles himself will be exalted" (Luke 18:14).

This story never really happened. This story has happened a thousand times.

How can it be that the tax collector in Jesus's parable walks away justified? The answer lies in what his brief statement teaches. Because Jesus is the author, each word has been chosen and arranged with perfect intent:

"God, have mercy on me, a sinner."

Note the word picture the man's statement creates. God at one end of the sentence, a sinner at the other, mercy in between. But there's more to this request for mercy. The specific word Jesus chooses for "have mercy on me" is the verb form of the word we translate as "mercy seat." Jesus's audience for his story knew that the mercy seat was the covering on the ark of the covenant. The ark was located in the Most Holy Place, designed to represent a throne. Inside the ark was the "testimony"—the Ten Commandments, the implements of God's justice. Once a year the high priest sprinkled the mercy seat with the blood of an innocent, spotless sacrifice to atone for the sins of the people.

In essence, the tax collector cries out, "God, be *mercy-seated* toward me, a sinner." What lands on our modern ears as a scarcity of words is actually a perfectly calibrated plea. The tax collector, in all his insufficiency of righteousness and speech, casts himself on the mercy of atoning blood, interposing itself between him and God.[2]

This story never really happened. This story has happened a thousand times.

It is the picture of our salvation. The tax collector's cry is the cry of all who recognize that the only basis by which they can approach a holy God is the shed blood of an innocent Lamb.

James, the brother of Jesus, echoes this idea when he reminds us that "mercy triumphs over judgment" (James 2:13). Or, more literally, "mercy exalts itself over judgment." I suspect James, like Jesus, is also sketching a word picture, recalling that golden throne of the ark in the Most Holy Place. The psalmist describes God's justice as the foundation of his throne (Ps. 89:14). See there, the Ten Commandments laid in the base of the ark. But God does not take his seat on justice. No, he takes his seat on mercy. At the completion of the tabernacle, Moses obeyed God's commands to the letter with regard to its assembly: "He took the testimony and put it into the ark . . . and set the mercy seat above on the ark" (Ex. 40:20).

Gaze on the image and heed its lesson. Mercy exalts itself above judgment. Where the law would condemn, mercy triumphs.

In View of God's Mercy

How's my driving? Thanks for asking. Since that speeding ticket, I don't drive the way I used to. Every time I'm tempted to rush through a yellow light, my conscience is pricked. I pay attention with a vigilance I used to lack, unwilling that Jeff's name should bear further reproach because of my lawbreaking. Mercy has that effect on its recipients. It changes the way we live.

Having spoken at length of the nature and depth of God's mercy to both Jew and Gentile, the apostle Paul concludes this: "Therefore, I urge you, brothers and sisters, *in view of God's mercy*, to offer your bodies as a living sacrifice, holy and pleasing to God—this is your true and proper worship" (Rom. 12:1 NIV).

As the children of God, as those toward whom he has been mercy-seated, we now live with mercy always in view. The result of this perspective is the sacrificial laying down of our lives for others. As far as we are able, we allow mercy to triumph over judgment.

Mercy means relieving suffering, both physical and spiritual. In view of God's mercy, we sacrifice our own bodily comfort that others might find relief in their lack. We do this for those we love, certainly. But we also do this for those to whom we bear no obligation, according to the world, but to whom, according to the cross, we bear an enormous obligation. Rather than measure ourselves against the broken and the desperate and finding ourselves more righteous than they, we remember our lowly estate apart from Christ and offer the cup of mercy to their lips.

Mercy also means forgiving as we have been forgiven. In view of God's mercy, we sacrifice our bitterness and grudge-bearing for the sake of extending forgiveness. We also sacrifice our legitimate hurts—the pain of unfair rejection or the sorrow of a wound unjustly received. We entrust them to God, remembering that Christ endured the same from us and for us, and to a much greater degree.

The natural question may arise: "How many times must I forgive?" We are not left to wonder. Peter once asked the same question of Jesus. Having some knowledge of the generous mercy of God, he frames his question in such a way that he no doubt expects Jesus to commend him: "Lord, how often will my brother sin against me, and I forgive him? As many as seven times?" (Matt. 18:21).

The rabbis of Peter's day taught that a generous mercy entailed forgiving up to three times, but no more. Peter, rather grandiosely, suggests a higher number than the rabbis, and a symbolic one—the number seven is frequently used in the Old Testament to signify perfection or completeness. Jesus responds with a call to generous mercy that extends farther than Peter would ever contemplate: "I do not say to you [forgive] seven times, but seventy-seven times" (Matt. 18:22).

Jesus amplifies Peter's symbolic number. He multiplies it by ten and adds another seven for good measure: $7 \times 10 + 7$. He combines Peter's 7 of completeness with the number 10, which also signifies completeness. How many times should we forgive? $7 \times 10 + 7$. Completely times completely plus completely. He follows his statement with a parable of a man who, after being forgiven an astronomical debt, turns and treats mercilessly the man who owes him a minor debt. The point is clear: Jesus tells Peter to forgive as he has been forgiven. To the uttermost, as God has forgiven us.[3]

Peter himself would be immortalized in Scripture for denying Jesus three times in one night alone. Three absolutions would not be enough. Nor would seven. No, only a generous mercy, a lavish mercy, would do.

Withholding mercy from others reveals that we do not recognize what we ourselves have received. The vast mercy of God has fallen from our view. We must obey the will of God for our lives to "be merciful, even as your Father is merciful" (Luke 6:36).

Wise Mercy

Forgiving lavishly does not mean that we continue to place ourselves in harm's way. The Bible takes great pains to address the dangers of keeping company with those who perpetually harm others. Those who learn nothing from their past mistakes are termed fools. While we may forgive the fool for hurting us, we do not give the fool unlimited opportunity to hurt us again. To do so would be to act foolishly ourselves. When Jesus extends mercy in the Gospels, he always does so with an implicit or explicit "Go and sin no more." When our offender persists in sinning against us, we are wise to put boundaries in place. Doing so is itself an act of mercy toward the offender. By limiting his opportunity to sin against us, we spare him further guilt before God. Mercy never requires submission to abuse, whether spiritual, verbal, emotional, or physical.

Yes, Jesus endured all of these for the sake of atoning for our sins. But we are not him. In everything he endured, he was never a victim. A victim is someone who is overpowered against her will by a more powerful person. We can and will be victimized, and the less power we have, the more frequently we are likely to be. This is why the Bible makes clear our responsibility to care for the widow and orphan. Women and children, who frequently lack power in society, are more easily victimized and, statistics show, more frequently victimized. Jesus did not ever, for one instant of the incarnation, lack power. If he is a victim, he is not a Savior. Having access to limitless power, he willingly laid down his life. We follow his example of extending mercy, but we do so as those capable of being victimized. We forgive to the uttermost, but we do not enable or condone continuing victimization—ours or someone else's.

Mercy's Table

Often, those to whom we most need to extend mercy and forgiveness are unaware of the injury they have caused. Often, they perceive no need to ask our forgiveness. It is hard to extend mercy to the merciless. It is hard to say with Jesus, "Father, forgive them, for they know not what they do" (Luke 23:34). Even when we are able to do so, we find that, over time, old hurts can resurrect themselves. This is why God continually prepares a table for us in the presence of our enemies. When the old enemy of unforgiveness raises its head, we remember that our own heads have been anointed with the oil of gladness. We approach again the table of our own forgiveness.

We must never forget that Jesus instituted a table of mercy *on the night in which he was betrayed.* On that night, he said of the bread, "This is my body." On that night, he said of the wine, "This is my blood."

> Bread of the world in mercy broken,
> Wine of the soul in mercy shed,
> by whom the words of life were spoken,
> and in whose death our sins are dead:
> look on the heart by sorrow broken;
> look on the tears by sinners shed;
> so may your feast become the token
> that by your grace our souls are fed. (Reginald Heber, 1827)

Come to the table in view of God's mercy. Come once. Come again. How many times is the table of his body and blood spread before you? Forgive that many times. Forgive, and keep forgiving. He presented his body as a sacrifice. Now present yours, as your reasonable act of worship (Rom. 12:1). Mercy triumphs over judgment.

Blessed are the merciful, for they shall receive mercy.

Blessed are the merciful, for they have received mercy.

Blessed are the merciful, for the mercy they have received is without end.

Verses for Meditation

Psalm 51:1

Psalm 119:156

Proverbs 28:13
Lamentations 3:22–23
Zechariah 7:8–10
Luke 6:35–36
Titus 3:4–6

Questions for Reflection

1. Are you more like the Pharisee or the tax collector in Jesus's story? How aware are you of your desperate need for mercy? What prevents you from recognizing your need and confessing it more fervently?

2. Describe a time in your life when you showed mercy by forgiving someone who had not asked for your forgiveness (even if that person was unaware of it). What was the result? What did you learn about being a follower of Christ?

3. Toward whom is it easiest for you to show compassion? Toward whom is it hardest? What is the difference between those two relationships or types of people that causes you to respond differently to them? How does God view them?

4. How should a desire to grow in mercy impact our relationship with God positively? How should it impact our relationships with others positively? Give a specific example of each.

Pray

Write a prayer to God thanking him for the lavish mercy that is yours in Christ. Ask him to help you be merciful as he is merciful. Ask him to make you an instrument of active compassion for those bound by suffering and sin. Thank him for preparing a table for you, at which new mercies are always waiting.

6

God Most Gracious

'Twas grace that taught my heart to fear,
And grace my fears relieved.

John Newton, 1779

I pull up to the section of the curb that is painted cornflower blue, sloping gently to the parking lot. I lift her walker from the back of the car and set it next to the passenger door so she can find her balance as she stands. Her outfit is perfectly matched, neat, and paired with a necklace she bought at a museum gift shop years ago. Her lips are petal pink, the lipstick shade consistent with virtually every childhood memory I have of her. She emerges, smiling at me, grasping the handles of the walker, the scent of honeysuckle and lilac accompanying her movements. I know what is next. It is the lifelong script of our mother-daughter partings, both the momentous and the ordinary. I lean in to receive the impression of her petal pink benediction on my cheek. "I love you!" I say. She responds: "I love you more!"

I watch her make her way carefully through the door of her apartment building and remember how that response used to irritate a teenaged version of me. Why not just say, "I love you, too"? It's not a competition. But when I became a mother myself, I realized that she was not trying to one-up me. She was simply acknowledging a fact: parents love their children more than children love their parents. They love more for the plain reason that they love longest—having begun to love before the child is born, and then loving that child from an adult vantage point—with the full force of adult understanding of the world, of danger and loss, of grief and joy and expectancy and regret. Our own happiness intertwines inseparably with theirs. Even when they are "grown and flown," our hearts fly with them.

Grace Abundant

As impossible as it is to understand the sisters of grace and mercy without justice, it would be equally impossible to speak of grace apart from love. Love expresses itself in grace. The grace of God is his unmerited favor, but to define it merely as such is to miss the extravagant nature of that favor. Jesus declared that he had come not just that we would have life, but abundant life (John 10:10). He purchased for us not just a merciful reprieve from the penalty of death, but an introduction into a life of grace beyond measure.

We come to our heavenly Father much like the prodigal son, able only to utter a cry for mercy, hoping somehow we will not get what we deserve, unable to lift our eyes to the prospect of grace—that we would receive far more than we deserve. But our Father responds with more than we could ask or imagine (Eph. 3:20). His grace is the expression of his love toward sinners, a demonstration of favor that is not merely adequate, but abundant. It is the simple acknowledgment of a parental fact: "I love you more."

Though as earthly parents our own happiness is bound to that of our children, our heavenly Father is unbound by his children in any regard. He desires us to flourish and delights when we do, but he does not need us to flourish. Because he depends on us for nothing, his grace is given freely and unconditionally. By definition grace cannot be earned, which is good, because we have no righteousness of our own with which to secure any good thing from him. We cannot convince him to give it through winning arguments, as he knows every argument already—the true and the false. We cannot coerce him to give it because he is always stronger than we. This makes him a better parent than our earthly parents, a clear-sighted parent knowing "much more" how to give good things to those who ask (Matt. 7:11). He bestows grace as he pleases, and he does so perfectly.

Abundance. Initially, grace is unasked for and undesired. God in his sovereignty extends grace to us before we can even contemplate its possibility or its worth. Eternally, grace is unearned and undeserved. We grow to recognize it for what it is, and we even become increasingly bold to ask for it in greater measure. But the moment we begin to ask out of a sense of entitlement, we contaminate grace. To demand it is to defile it. In doing so, we take on the role of the prodigal's older brother, grown so accustomed to abundance that he believes it is his by right rather than by gift.

Grace Eternal

But let us turn our attention from fractious brothers to those close-knit sisters, mercy and grace. Even more than mercy, grace is perceived to be a New Testament concept, so closely is it connected to the person of Christ. We read in John's Gospel that "the law was given through Moses; grace and truth came through Jesus Christ" (John 1:17). It is easy to slip into thinking that grace must not have operated prior to Jesus's incarnation. But because he is the eternal Son of God, Christians understand that all believers are saved by grace through faith alone, those in the Old Testament placing their faith in a future demonstration of that grace at Calvary, those in the New Testament placing their faith in it as a historical fact. A. W. Tozer describes the eternal nature of grace:

> No one was ever saved other than by grace, from Abel to the present moment. Since mankind was banished from the eastward Garden, none has ever returned to the divine favor except through the sheer goodness of God. And wherever grace found any man it was always by Jesus Christ. Grace indeed came by Jesus Christ, but it did not wait for His birth in the manger or His death on the cross before it became operative. Christ is the Lamb slain from the foundation of the world. The first man in human history to be reinstated in the fellowship of God came through faith in Christ. In olden times men looked forward to Christ's redeeming work; in later times they gaze back upon it, but always they came and they come by grace, through faith.[1]

No sooner does sin enter the garden than grace appears, clothing Adam and Eve in animal skins Gods himself supplies. It is God who provides the first sacrifice, as it is God who provides the last. Grace from the garden to Golgotha. Grace from Golgotha to this generation. *And grace shall lead us home.*

How does grace lead us home? She does not take the broad and beaten path, but the narrow one. But it is the path of abundance, nonetheless, its trail markers placed by the teachings and example of Christ himself. Jesus does more than inaugurate the abundant life of grace, he defines it and demonstrates it. Perhaps nowhere do we hear abundance expounded by Jesus as clearly as the day he spoke of it seated on a mountainside, surrounded by his followers.

Abundantly Blessed

Those followers, like you and me, no doubt sat before Jesus with their own working definitions for the abundant life. And no doubt they defined it not much differently than we do today; the abundant life is one of power, status, acceptance, and wealth. Social media bears daily evidence to the enduring nature of this definition:

"Great vacation in Hawaii with the family. #blessed"

"Our son Ryan got a full ride to CSU! #blessed"

"Humbled and grateful to have been named top producer at my company. #blessed"

If the disciples had used social media, these same kinds of statements would have shown up in their accounts, perhaps populated with reports about the size of their fishing fleet or a Mitzvah celebration. But then they meet Jesus, and I wonder if they might have tweeted something like this: "Honored to join the startup team for the kingdom of heaven! #blessed."

Like us, they may have mistaken proximity with the Messiah as a means to an abundance of power, status, acceptance, or wealth. So, Jesus takes his seat and opens his mouth to point them toward the true nature of abundant living.

Blessed are the poor in spirit, those who mourn, the meek, those who hunger and thirst for righteousness.

Blessed are the merciful, the pure in heart, the peacemakers, those who are persecuted for righteousness' sake.

Theirs is the kingdom. Theirs is the life abundant.

Do you understand the poverty of your spirit? You are blessed. Do you grieve over your sin? You are blessed. Have you learned to submit your will to God and to crave what is true? You are blessed beyond measure. Poverty, grief, meekness, and famine usher us into the life of abundance as surely as they did the Israelites fresh from Egypt's grasp. Mercy, purity, peace, and persecution mark the daily life of abundance as surely as they marked the life of our Savior.

Contrary to what the world would say, Jesus describes the abundant life as the life lived in humility. As his brother James would later say, "God opposes the proud but gives grace to the humble" (James 4:6; cf. Prov. 3:34). God gives grace to those who embrace this abundant life, and he does so that we may live it as Christ did. God's unmerited favor fuels our sanctification. It serves two purposes in the lives of those who would walk humbly with their God: it teaches them and it strengthens them.

Taught by Grace

The apostle Paul explains to Titus the teaching role of grace in the life of the Christ-follower:

> For the grace of God has appeared that offers salvation to all people. It teaches us to say "No" to ungodliness and worldly passions, and to live self-controlled, upright and godly lives in this present age, while we wait for the blessed hope—the appearing of the glory of our great God and Savior, Jesus Christ, who gave himself for us to redeem us from all wickedness and to purify for himself a people that are his very own, eager to do what is good. (Titus 2:11–14 NIV)

Don't miss this: grace teaches us to heed God's moral law. The moral law instructs us in what is displeasing (ungodliness and worldly passions) and pleasing (self-controlled, upright, and godly lives) to God. Apart from grace, we were unable to obey it. As recipients of grace, we are both capable of obedience and commanded to obedience—to eager obedience, to be precise. Whereas the law pointed us to our need for grace, now grace points us to our need for the law. Grace enables us to humbly submit to God's good government. And God gives grace to the humble that they may do just that.

The ongoing importance of the law in sanctification explains why Jesus warned so forcefully against relaxing its commands or teaching others to do so (Matt. 5:19). If grace is seen only as a free gift to cover our sins and not also as a means to growing in holiness, we will grow lax in our obedience. Dietrich Bonhoeffer points to this tendency in his well-known discussion of "cheap grace":

> Grace is represented as the Church's inexhaustible treasury, from which she showers blessings with generous hands, without asking questions or fixing limits. Grace without price; grace without cost! The essence of grace, we suppose, is that the account has been paid in advance; and, because it has been paid, everything can be had for nothing. . . . In such a Church the world finds a cheap covering for its sins; no contrition is required, still less any real desire to be delivered from sin. Cheap grace therefore amounts to a denial of the living Word of God, in fact, a denial of the Incarnation of the Word of God.
>
> Cheap grace means the justification of sin without the justification of the sinner. Grace alone does everything they say, and so everything can remain as it was before. "All for sin could not atone." Well, then, let the Christian live like the rest of the world, let him model himself on the world's standards in every sphere of life, and not presumptuously

aspire to live a different life under grace from his old life under sin.[2]

It will not do for believers to relax the law, and thereby teach others that such a practice is safe. We can have no benign tolerance of the "smaller sins" about which we are warned: gossip, meddling, shading the truth, vanity, boasting, envy—those sins we may reckon as affordable, perhaps even inconsequential. To do so is to invite instability into our walk and our witness by committing the error of those who reject the law: "You therefore, beloved, knowing this beforehand, take care that you are not carried away with the error of lawless people and lose your own stability. But grow in the grace and knowledge of our Lord and Savior Jesus Christ" (2 Pet. 3:17–18).

Instead of shrinking into lawlessness, we are to grow in grace and truth, after the pattern of Christ, full of grace and truth. Grace teaches us to say no to ungodliness and yes to godliness. With regard to our justification, grace invites us to relax from our striving to earn what is a free gift. With regard to our sanctification, grace instructs us to reject the error of lawless people, that we may grow in grace. Grace begets grace. Another abundance.

Strengthened by Grace

If all this talk of being trained by grace to obey has made you feel a little unequal to the task, take heart. Grace does not just teach us to renounce ungodliness, it also strengthens us to do so.

In his parting words to the elders of the Ephesian church, Paul commends them to God "and to the word of his grace, which is able to build you up and to give you the inheritance among all those who are sanctified" (Acts 20:32). Similarly, both Hebrews 13:9 and 2 Timothy 2:1 speak of being strengthened by grace for the purpose of faithful obedience. Grace builds us up and strengthens us, that we might live holy lives in accordance with the law.

D. A. Carson speaks of sanctification as "grace-driven effort."[3] We strive toward holiness not in our own strength alone, but by the power of grace. In what sense does grace empower us? We have been given the gracious gift of the Spirit of God as our helper in all these things. Zechariah 12:10 and Hebrews 10:29 call him "the Spirit of grace."

The Spirit of grace is both a gracious gift and a gracious gift-giver. He gives "the Spirit of wisdom and understanding, the Spirit of counsel and might, the Spirit of knowledge and the fear of the LORD" (Isa. 11:2). And all of these are lavish gifts of grace, to be used by those who receive them "to serve one another, as good stewards of God's varied grace" (1 Pet. 4:10).

Those who enjoy such abundance can afford to deal abundantly with others. They no longer live a bare minimum life with regard to their neighbors, always looking for ways to minimize what neighborliness might require of them. Instead, they recognize, in a way they once did not, the full implications of the Law and the Prophets: "Do to others as you would have them do to you" (Matt. 7:12 NIV). So clearly valuable is the moral imperative of this statement that even those outside the Christian faith have adopted it as "the Golden Rule." But without an understanding of the abundant nature of grace, even the Golden Rule can be employed from a bare minimum perspective.

Humble Pie

Nothing makes me more aware of the way I want to be treated than when I'm staring down one remaining piece of coconut cream pie. It is my favorite pie to make and to eat. When I see that there is only one piece to be had, my first thought is always to inhale it secretly in the corner. It takes every ounce of will-power to ask if anyone else would like it. I usually size it up to see if it can be subdivided in some equitable way. Even if I successfully offer and serve it to someone else, I'm consumed with the nobility of my deprivation and am likely to reward myself with half a package of Oreos as a consolation prize.

Scarcity has a way of revealing our true understanding of the Golden Rule. Here's the bare truth: when there is one piece of pie, I don't want to deny myself and bless someone else with it, and I don't want to divide it equitably. I want the whole piece. And that's precisely why I should give the whole piece to someone else—because in doing so, I fulfill the Golden Rule. Yes, at bare minimum I want to be treated fairly by others. But what I really want is to be treated preferentially.

My love of preferential treatment displays itself in a thousand ways. I want the best concert seats, the best parking spot, the upgrade to first class, the most comfortable seat in the living room, the biggest serving of pie, the last serving of pie, all the pie all the time. Giving someone else the preferential treatment that I want requires humility. But God gives grace to the humble. Any time we dine on humble pie, we can be certain it will be accompanied by an oversized dollop of grace.

Christians should not have a reputation for being merely fair. We should have a reputation for playing favorites with everyone except ourselves. As those who have received abundant grace, we do good in abundance: "And God is able to make all grace abound to you, so that having all sufficiency in all things at all times, you may abound in every good work" (2 Cor. 9:8).

Our lives should demonstrate that there is no such thing as scarcity when you are a child of God, that our heavenly Father has given all that is needful and much more than we could ask or imagine. We should be recognized as peddlers in abundance. We should be known as the people who respond to "I hate you" with "I love you," and as the people who respond to "I love you" with "I love you more."

What is the will of God for your life? That you may have life, and that you may have it abundantly. That you may show preference to others, even as it has been shown to you in Christ. And that you would walk the narrow path, daily assured by the grace you received at the cross and daily strengthened by the grace you receive for every step forward toward holiness.

Verses for Meditation
Psalm 116:5–9
Psalm 145:8
2 Corinthians 9:8
Ephesians 1:3–10
Titus 2:11–14

Questions for Reflection
1. In what area of your life are you like the prodigal son, believing your sin (past or present) to be beyond the reach of grace? How would God respond to your evaluation of your sin?

2. Read through the Beatitudes in Matthew 5:2–12. How does the way Jesus describes the abundant life of a Christ-follower challenge your own conception of what it means to be blessed? How have you known his description to be truer than how the world defines abundant life?

3. Describe a time in your life when you fulfilled the Golden Rule by showing preferential treatment to a difficult person. What was the result? What did you learn about being a follower of Christ?

4. How should a desire to grow in grace impact our relationship with God positively? How should it impact our relationships with others positively? Give a specific example of each.

Pray

Write a prayer to God thanking him for the abundant life of grace that is yours in Christ. Ask him to help you be gracious as he is gracious. Ask him to help you deal generously with others, as one who has been dealt generously with by him. Thank him for making a way through Christ for you to receive grace upon grace.

7

God Most Faithful

All I have needed thy hand hath provided—
Great is thy faithfulness, Lord, unto me!

Thomas Chisholm, 1923

On a September afternoon in 1870, a party of nine explorers, eight army escorts, and two cooks made its way by horseback along the Firehole River in an untamed corner of Wyoming. Their task was to explore the mountains and valleys of an ancient volcano crater, an area known for geothermal activity. Nathaniel P. Langford, a member of the expedition, later recounted what met their gaze that September day:

> Judge, then, what must have been our astonishment, as we entered the basin at mid-afternoon of our second day's travel, to see in the clear sunlight, at no great distance, an immense volume of clear, sparkling water projected into the air to the height of one hundred and twenty-five feet. "Geysers! geysers!" exclaimed one of our company, and,

spurring our jaded horses, we soon gathered around this wonderful phenomenon. It was indeed a perfect geyser. The aperture through which the jet was projected was an irregular oval, three feet by seven in diameter. . . . It spouted at regular intervals nine times during our stay, the columns of boiling water being thrown from ninety to one hundred and twenty-five feet at each discharge, which lasted from fifteen to twenty minutes. We gave it the name of "Old Faithful."[1]

One of the best-known features of what is now Yellowstone National Park, Old Faithful earned its name for the predictability of its eruptions, a predictability that continues to this day and no doubt had been evidenced for centuries before—long before there were benches for spectators, a visitor's center, or published schedules of its next display. In Langford's day, the only way to witness Old Faithful was to travel to Wyoming, a trip requiring expense, difficulty, time, and danger. But today, thanks to a webcam and the generosity of the National Park Service, anyone with internet access can watch the geyser erupt in real time. The faithfulness of Old Faithful can now be witnessed by whoever takes the time to view it.

The Only Faithful

In the opening lines of Psalm 90, Moses declares, "Before the mountains were brought forth, or ever you had formed the earth and the world, from everlasting to everlasting you are God" (v. 2). Eternally, God has been God, unchanging in all his attributes.

Before the volcanic cataclysm that raised the mountains of Wyoming, there was an eternally faithful God, steadfast in all his ways, devoted to utter consistency between his words and his deeds.

From of old no one has heard
  or perceived by the ear,
no eye has seen a God besides you,
  who acts for those who wait for him. (Isa. 64:4)

In his faithfulness "from of old," God does what he says he will do, always. Those he saves, he is able to save to the uttermost, so complete is his faithfulness. He is faithful to his children because he cannot be unfaithful to himself. He is incapable of infidelity on any level.

No human we know is consistently faithful. The most steadfast person we have ever known has or will let us down. The Bible clearly attests to this, choosing to present the stories of its "heroes" in all their unvarnished glory. The list of faithful men and women recorded in Hebrews 11 includes among its ranks murderers and liars, scoffers, cowards, and bullies—even the most admirable among them knew what it was to break a trust. Only God is fully faithful. Only God is surpassingly steadfast.

The faithfulness of God is both a comfort to his children and a terror to those who oppose him:

> Know therefore that the LORD your God is God, the faithful God who keeps covenant and steadfast love with those who love him and keep his commandments, to a thousand generations, and repays to their face those who hate him, by destroying them. He will not be slack with one who hates him. He will repay him to his face. (Deut. 7:9–10)

Too often we are tempted to quote only the first part of Moses's words to Israel, so uncomfortable are we with God's wrath. But God is faithful to execute justice on those who reject him, just as he is faithful to maintain steadfast love toward those whom he has received. He blesses those he has said he will bless, and he curses those he has said he will curse. To worship God as wholly faithful, we must endeavor to hold both of these expressions of faithfulness in view. We need a God who is wholly faithful. When the children of God choose to forget the terror of divine judgment, they fashion God in their own image. By forgetting his faithfulness to judge, they forget him altogether.

Reminders of Faithfulness

God knows our tendency toward forgetfulness. Like a loving parent leaving a trail of sticky note reminders for a child, throughout history God has taken measures to ensure that his children would remember his faithfulness. He established the Sabbath as a remembrance of his creative work. He commanded the raising of memorial stones when Joshua led Israel across the Jordan into the Promised Land. He instituted feast days in the Jewish calendar as memory aids of his past faithfulness to Israel. Circumcision was a sign by which to remember God's covenant with Abraham, just as baptism and the Lord's Supper serve as remembrances of the new covenant.

The seasons themselves bear witness to the steadfastness of God, as does the rising and setting of the sun. Each day proclaims the truth of God's promise to Noah, "As long as the earth endures, seedtime and harvest, cold and heat, summer and winter, day and night will never cease" (Gen. 8:22 NIV). The manifold witness of nature testifies to a God who is great in faithfulness.

The Bible is our great Ebenezer, a memorial stone to the faithfulness of God, carefully recorded and preserved for his children. When we grow forgetful of God, or when we question whether God has forgotten us, we can turn there to gaze on his steadfast love to all generations. Unlike generations before us, we have unprecedented access to this priceless reminder. Bibles by the billions, literally. And every copy, from the dog-eared to the disregarded, is whispering, "Remember." Remember the God who remembers you.

Believers whose Bibles are worn have known their need of its message. To them, reading its pages is not just a dutiful practice but a delightful privilege. They know that between its covers a glorious truth is repeated for their great benefit: God is worthy of our trust.

When we spend time in the Bible, our lives begin to bear witness to its faithful message. We ourselves become stones of remembrance for those around us, giving faithful testimony that God is worthy of our trust, no matter what.

Faithful in Trial

No life is free of trial. But God's Word assures us that, no matter what trying circumstance we find ourselves in, he never leaves us or forsakes us (Heb. 13:5). He is the solid rock in the storms of life, the sure foundation. When trials beset us, we can know that our faithful God has not abandoned us. Though we may not be able to perceive his goodness and lovingkindness in the moment, we can rely on the record of his past faithfulness as evidence that we can count on him in the present.

After being sold into slavery by his own brothers, Joseph endured years of imprisonment and exile. Even when God elevated him to second-in-command of all of Egypt, giving him the vision and ability to deliver thousands from starvation during a long famine, he continued to carry the great sorrow of his past. When at last God reconciled him to his family, he was able to say, "As for you, you meant evil against me, but God meant it for good, to bring it about that many people should be kept alive, as they are today" (Gen. 50:20).

Joseph illustrates for us what James promises about trials:

Consider it pure joy, my brothers and sisters, whenever you face trials of many kinds, because you know that the testing of your faith produces perseverance. Let perseverance finish its work so that you may be mature and complete, not lacking anything. (James 1:2–4 NIV)

Trials always prove the faithfulness of God, though it may take years to see. And as they prove the faithfulness of God, they produce faithfulness in us. Joseph witnessed glimpses of God's faithfulness through the long years of his testing, and was ultimately able to testify that God used his personal suffering to save many from starvation. The faithful suffering of one accomplished the salvation of many. Joseph's faithfulness in trial pointed to Christ.

When we meet trials, we do not rejoice in the suffering they bring but in the faithfulness of God to use them to shape us, that we might become like Christ. God is faithful in the midst of trial, and faithful in the aftermath of trial to work all things for our good.

Faithful in Temptation

Trials bring us to our knees and remind us of our limits. They reorient us toward God. But they are not the only difficulty God uses to train us in righteousness. God also uses temptation to shape us. James reminds us that God does not tempt us and is himself unable to be tempted (James 1:13). This makes sense when we consider his omniscience. Whereas we are happy to entertain the suggestion of sin, to God it is laughable. He knows every outcome of every scenario. He cannot be fooled into thinking sin will end well. We, on the other hand, allow ourselves to weigh the costs and benefits (as if there could be any benefit to sin). We tell ourselves, as Adam and Eve did, that perhaps God is holding out on us. Perhaps he wants to keep good gifts from us, to cheat us of something. Every entertainment of temptation questions the goodness of God.

Yet, even as we tinker with the thought that God is a liar and a cheat, he acts toward us in steadfast love: "No temptation has overtaken you that is not common to man. God is faithful, and he will not let you be tempted beyond your ability, but with the temptation he will also provide the way of escape, that you may be able to endure it" (1 Cor. 10:13).

Take note that God provides the way of escape *in faithfulness*. Even as we contemplate unfaithfulness to him, he stands faithfully pointing the way to salvation.

Then consider the comfort that all temptation is *common*. We want to believe that it is uncommon, that the sin we give in to was something God did not see coming, that we face a dilemma no one before us has ever had to face. We want to tell ourselves that we have sinned because we faced an exceptional temptation that dragged us away. But James tells us that our own desires are what do the dragging (James 1:14). The temptation itself is common. As old as time. A complete yawner to the Almighty. Which means that providing a way of escape does not require ingenuity on his part. The way of escape is as common as the temptation itself: Listen to the Holy Spirit. Trust that God is not a liar. Choose the path of righteousness.

All temptation is common. All temptation is escapable. Every believer has the ability to overcome it.

Like a muscle that gains strength over repeated workouts, so our ability to turn from temptation grows stronger with repeated practice. In order to lift a very heavy weight, a weightlifter starts with smaller weights and builds up strength over time. When we are faithful to God in smaller temptations, we build strength to face the bigger ones. No one indulges an explosive fit of anger who has not first indulged a thousand smaller aggressions. If we habitually flee from the temptation to commit minor sins of anger and selfishness, we are less likely to fall for temptation to greater sins of anger and selfishness. If we habitually excuse smaller sins, we should not be surprised to find ourselves increasingly entangled in larger ones.

Jesus taught that those who are faithful in small things will be faithful in big things (Luke 16:10). Behind every temptation, great or small, stands the faithfulness of God eager to provide a way of escape. When we answer his faithfulness with our faithfulness, temptation loses both its glitter and its brawn.

Faithful in Forgiveness

Both trials and temptation teach us the faithfulness of God and train us in reciprocal faithfulness. But perhaps most reassuring of all is the faithfulness he shows in his seventy-times-seven forgiveness of sin.

In our discussion of God as just, we contemplated the unexpected role of justice in the forgiveness of our sins. Now, let us reflect on the incomprehensible depth of his faithfulness in forgiveness. John tells us, "If we confess our sins, he is faithful and just to forgive us our sins and to cleanse us from all unrighteousness" (1 John 1:9). When we are faithful to confess, he is faithful to forgive. No matter how many times we confess new sin, no matter how many times we confess repeated sin, God is faithful to forgive. The longer we live the life of faith, the greater our awareness of sin will grow. We will never reach the end of our confession this side of heaven, nor will we ever reach the end of his faithfulness to meet our confession with forgiveness.

But we will go to our graves with unconfessed sin. We will die still blind to areas of sinfulness, whether past or present. Is God faithful to forgive those sins, as well? Once again, God's omniscience offers assurance of his faithfulness. Though we do not know all our sins, he does.

Christ's atoning death covers all our sin, even the sin we are oblivious to. David prayed to God, "But who can discern their own errors? Forgive my hidden faults" (Ps. 19:12 NIV). Though we lack the ability to fully discern the extent of our sin, the God who knows every one of them is faithful to forgive them all.

Faithful to the Finish

The Bible records God's faithfulness to do exactly what he says he will do. His promise to make Abraham a great nation came to pass. His promise to bring Israel out of Egypt came to pass. His promise to send a deliverer came to pass, just as he had said. Not all that he has promised has come to pass yet, but it will in the fullness of time. He has promised us deliverance from sin. Though we see the good work of that deliverance taking place in us, it is not yet complete. But because God holds all power, he is able to do all that he promises, and none can stay his hand. This is why the Christian defines hope as more than just wishful optimism.

Because of God's limitless power and unshakeable faithfulness, the hope we have in him is hope with certainty. We do not hope in his promises with our fingers crossed behind our backs. Rather, we hope as those who know he has certainly been faithful in the past and will certainly be faithful to the end. We can hope with certainty that "he who began a good work in you will bring it to completion at the day of Jesus Christ" (Phil. 1:6).

He has promised that the day of Jesus Christ will come. And come it certainly will. On a day still future, the Savior will return, seated on a white horse, bearing the name Faithful and True (Rev. 19:11). Though we await that day amid hardship, toil, and temptation, we can hope with certainty that a thousand years are as a day to God. At just the right time, the heavens will surely split. Therefore, "Let us hold fast the confession of our hope without wavering, for he who promised is faithful" (Heb. 10:23).

Faithful as He Is Faithful

God is faithful to do what he says he will do. As far as it is possible with us, we should be the same. We should reciprocate his faithfulness to us with faithfulness toward him. We should reflect his faithfulness to us with faithfulness toward others. Jesus Christ is the perfect expression of God's faithfulness toward humankind, as well as the perfect expression of human faithfulness toward God and others. His example shows us the way of faithfulness.

In Psalm 119:30 David says, "I have chosen the way of faithfulness; I set your rules before me." The life of faithfulness is one in which we daily choose to place our hope in God, with every ounce of certainty that he will not fail us. We choose the way of faithfulness, though we know it will be marked by trials and temptation. We choose it in matters large and small. We use our time faithfully, not squandering it as those who serve only themselves might do. We use our abilities faithfully, to bring glory to the One who gave them to us. We guard our thoughts faithfully, centering them on what is true, honest, just, pure, lovely. We use our words faithfully, to edify and encourage, to exhort and rebuke, to pray without ceasing.

We reflect on our reputation before others. Are we known as faithful in our marriages, our business dealings, our parenting, our volunteer commitments, our friendships, our charitable works? Do we do what we say we will do? Do we let our yes be yes and our no be no? Are we steadfast, though the culture tells us that relationships are disposable and life should be lived in the passion of the moment?

Ultimately, every act of faithfulness toward others is an act of faithfulness toward God himself. Though others may make commitments they have little intention of keeping, the children of God strive to prove that their word is their bond. They do so not to win the trust or approval of others, but because they long to be like Christ. They long to hear with their ears, "Well done, good and faithful servant."

God's will for your life is that you be faithful as he is faithful. Faithful to him. Faithful to others. Faithful in this moment. Faithful to the end. That which he wills, he also enables.

"Now may the God of peace himself sanctify you completely, and may your whole spirit and soul and body be kept blameless at the coming of our Lord Jesus Christ. He who calls you is faithful; he will surely do it" (1 Thess. 5:23–24).

Verses for Meditation

Numbers 23:19
Lamentations 3:22–23
Psalm 25:10
1 Thessalonians 5:23–24
Hebrews 10:19–23

Questions for Reflection

1. Who is the most faithful person you have ever known? List several specific ways you witnessed that person's faithfulness. How does his or her example point to the faithfulness of Christ?

2. How have you known God's faithfulness in trial? How did your time of trial produce perseverance?

3. How have you known God's faithfulness in temptation? How has he provided a way out in the past? What temptation (small or large) are you currently indulging? What wisdom does God's Word offer as a way out?

4. How should a desire to grow in faithfulness impact our relationship with God positively? How should it impact our relationships with others positively? Give a specific example of each.

Pray

Write a prayer to God thanking him for the faithfulness and steadfast love that is yours in Christ. Ask him to help you choose the way of faithfulness each day. Ask him to help you to be steadfast in trials, and to faithfully seek the way out of every temptation, great or small. Thank him for the faithful example of Christ, who shows us the way of faithfulness.

8

God Most Patient

Praise him for his grace and favor
To his people in distress.
Praise him still the same forever,
Slow to chide, and swift to bless.

Henry F. Lyte, 1834

My commute to the office (which is also my church) is not a difficult one. On a Sunday morning it can take as little as ten minutes,
if I hit the lights just right. But on a weekday morning it can take
more than twice that time because of the school zones. Even so, it
doesn't come close to the frustrating one-hour commute I drove
daily for several years when I lived and worked in Houston. I'm
thankful for that experience, because it taught me a perspective
on my current commute that allows me to enjoy it every day.

Except that it didn't do that at all. You would think that with
such an easy drive, I wouldn't find a school zone or two to be bur-
densome, but you would be wrong. On many mornings, I find myself questioning why schools insist on being built inconveniently

right in the middle of communities. It was on one such morning that my drive brought me into contact with another commute elongator: an elderly person driving well below the speed limit and changing lanes at will. As I hit the brakes to avoid hitting him, my eyes caught his Christian-fish-adorned bumper sticker: "Be patient. God isn't finished with me yet."

I regret that the message did not have the teaching effect this dear man may have hoped for.

To be human is to do battle daily with impatience. And battle it we must, because of the close connection between impatience and anger. In my experience, these two states are usually separated by about a nanosecond. Not surprisingly, the Bible communicates the idea of patience in the phrase "slow to anger." It is a phrase used first to describe God, but then repeatedly to describe the wise man. Anger itself is not necessarily sinful, but anger quickly kindled—the anger of impatience—is a hallmark of the fool.

We are familiar with the maxim that patience is a virtue, but it is a virtue rarely sought. The world's solution to the problem of impatience is not to develop patience, but to eliminate as many situations that require it as possible. We want what we want when we want it. We do not want to wait. Providers of goods and services devote themselves to the elimination of wait times to compete for our business and attention. Place an order on Amazon.com and receive it the same day. Fly an airline enough and you'll be rewarded with earlier boarding times and faster baggage service. Buy a FastPass at Disney and skip the lines. Get dinner from a drive-through window in a matter of minutes.

Need information? No problem. Gone are the days of waiting for answers to your existential questions about who starred in what movie or what the lyrics are to that Guns N' Roses song. Thanks to the internet, we are all trivia geniuses, do-it-yourself gurus, and gourmet chefs—experts on any topic after a few minutes of searching for the right video or article. Speaking of articles, *The Boston Globe* reported on a study that sought to determine how long internet users were willing to wait for a page to load before abandoning it. The answer: users began to bail after a two-second wait time. After five seconds, 25 percent of users had abandoned. At ten seconds, the number rose to 50 percent.[1] Luckily, the *Globe* article loaded in under five seconds, or these statistics would not be recorded here for your enjoyment.

Research shows that the average attention span has shrunk from twelve seconds in the year 2000 to eight seconds in 2015. This means our attention span is now officially shorter than that of a goldfish by a full second.[2] Not only is waiting something we avoid; it is something we are increasingly ill-equipped to do. This is problematic for all of us, but particularly for the Christ-follower, who is admonished repeatedly in Scripture to wait on the Lord, to bear with others, to be patient in affliction, and to be slow to anger. Christians are a people of delayed gratification, awaiting a future hope and forgoing comfort in the present. But we dwell among a people of instant gratification, and it is far too easy to bob along behind the goldfish than to swim against the current.

The Perfect Patience of God

When God first declares his character to Moses, he describes himself as slow to anger (Ex. 34:6), a trait that is then extolled in eight other Old Testament references. We simply cannot get away from the patience of God portrayed in the Bible. God is patient with his children with regard to their sin. He is patient to bear with us as we progress along the path of sanctification, forgiving our sins again and again. He is patient to work out our deliverance in good time. He is patient to await a harvest, and patient to bring in the sheaves in the fullness of time. Our God is "not slow to fulfill his promise as some count slowness, but is patient toward you, not wishing that any should perish, but that all should reach repentance" (2 Pet. 3:9).

God's patience is an expression of his love. When we explored the *agape* of God in chapter 2, we turned to 1 Corinthians 13 for help. The first descriptor given there for divine love? Love is patient. Love does not flee at the first sign that things could take a while, nor does it rage when things do not go its way. The love of God is patient, for better or for worse. It bears all things.

God's patience grows in beauty when framed by his omniscience. The slow anger of God is miraculous in the extreme, considering that he knows and daily witnesses every anger-inducing thing about us. We allow the most trifling annoyance to test our patience: the way someone chews, the dirty dish left on the counter, the forgotten turn signal. These minor perceived grievances invite our anger to rise. But God, against whom we have committed and continue to commit actual sins both small and great, bears with us patiently in the full knowledge of every single one of our offenses.

Do not miss the hope to be found in this: God's patience implies expectancy. He is waiting for resolution; the objects of his forbearance will not remain a source of frustration forever. Patiently, he is working in us to will and to do for his good pleasure. Patiently, he is working all things together for our good and for his glory.

Slow It Down

Since God abounds in patience, we should strive to be patient as well. It is not surprising that the Bible gives ample indication that patience is the path of wisdom. Four times in Proverbs the wise person is described as slow to anger:

> Whoever is slow to anger has great understanding, but he who has a hasty temper exalts folly. (Prov. 14:29)

> A hot-tempered man stirs up strife, but he who is slow to anger quiets contention. (Prov. 15:18)

> Whoever is slow to anger is better than the mighty, and he who rules his spirit than he who takes a city. (Prov. 16:32)

> Good sense makes one slow to anger, and it is his glory to overlook an offense. (Prov. 19:11)

In the New Testament, James succinctly reiterates the wisdom of the Old testament:

> My dear brothers and sisters, take note of this: Everyone should be quick to listen, slow to speak and slow to become angry, because human anger does not produce the righteousness that God desires. (James 1:19–20 NIV)

Impatience is the gateway to an easily kindled, unrighteous anger. As such, it deserves our careful consideration. What causes it? How can it be remedied?

Counting the Cost

Simply put, impatience results when we are bad at math. When we fail to count the cost of a particular endeavor or situation—the cost to our time, to our wallets, or to our egos—our patience ends up in the red. Any time you have ever thought, "This is harder than I expected" or "This is taking longer than I expected," you have faced the temptation to be impatient. And judging by how common impatience is, we are all bad at math.

Each of us has areas in our lives where, when it comes to estimating the cost, we miscalculate with vigor. We think marriage will give us bliss at a negligible cost. We think parenting will give our lives deep meaning at no expense. We think ministry or work will give us purpose without requiring much in return. Upon discovering the costly nature of a commitment, we lose patience and long only for it to improve or terminate in the shortest time possible.

We are bad at counting the cost of relationships, but we are also bad at counting the cost of trials. Most of us are observant enough to recognize the universal nature of suffering. We do not expect exemption, but we do tend to expect an express lane to the other side. We are surprised when our trial does not resolve in a timely manner after a round of faithful prayer and fasting. We are not good at math. We believe that the amount of time necessary for us to be made complete through suffering is much shorter than what God ordains.

If we can't be patient longer than five seconds for a website to load, we are not likely to weather a lengthy trial or sustain a hard relationship very well. Our anger will be easily kindled every time we don't get what we want when we want it. Amazon gets the package here the same day we order it. If we are not careful, we may begin to resent God's lack of concern to offer goods and services according to our timetable. We may even question his goodness. We may overlook the possibility that the waiting itself could be the good and perfect gift, delivered right to our doorstep.

It is often wryly observed that the secret to a happy life is holding low expectations. There is certainly some truth to the idea, though perhaps it is not low expectations, but right expectations we need most. Jesus spent considerable time establishing right expectations for what it would cost to be his disciples. He redefined blessedness, as we have seen, but he also reset expectations about how the world would respond to the message of the gospel, the amount of time it takes for righteousness to grow in us, and the amount of time it takes for the kingdom of heaven to come in fullness. To help us think rightly about these things, he told parables employing the language of harvest.

Most of us are far removed from agrarian settings. We lack the shared understanding of Jesus's original audience that farming takes time. Wheat harvests take months to sprout heads. Vineyards take several years to yield a vintage. A mustard seed takes decades to grow into a giant tree. We also lack a sense of the intense work farming involves. My limited experience with growing tomatoes involves daily visits to my plants thinking, "This is taking longer than I expected. This is harder than I expected."

So, when Jesus uses harvest images in his stories, the necessity of patience is assumed. It is also mentioned explicitly: "As for [the seed] in the good soil, they are those who, hearing the word, hold it fast in an honest and good heart, and bear fruit with patience"(Luke 8:15).

James, too, mentions patience in the context of harvest language: "Be patient, then, brothers and sisters, until the Lord's coming. See how the farmer waits for the land to yield its valuable crop, patiently waiting for the autumn and spring rains. You too, be patient" (James 5:7–8 NIV).

Why is the farmer patient? Because, by experience, he knows exactly how much time and what circumstances are necessary to yield a crop. He is good at counting the cost.

God is never impatient because he is very good at math. He never labors under a wrong expectation for what a circumstance or relationship will cost. He has never looked at the ongoing sin in your life and thought, "This is taking longer than I expected."

He has never looked upon the troubles of this world and thought, "This is harder than I expected." He is able to bear with us in our weakness because he understands the end from the beginning, and because he is able to not only count the cost of relationship, but to pay it.

The cost was a spotless Lamb.

Jesus Christ, who is the revelation of the patience of the Father, is also the perfect human example of patience.

The Patience of Christ

By the time I complete my morning commute and take a seat at my desk, I have committed the sin of impatience multiple times. By the time I make the commute home, I will have committed it multiple times more. Living shoulder to shoulder with sinners means our patience will be tried regularly. More often than not, our anger will be kindled and our response will not produce the righteousness that God desires.

Jesus Christ lived thirty-three years shoulder to shoulder with sinners, no doubt tempted constantly to sinful impatience and quick anger. Yet, the Bible records only two instances in which his anger manifested itself. Two. In thirty-three years. At every turn, he encountered people transgressing his Father's commands. To have expressed anger would have been justifiable, righteous. But even in expressing his righteous anger, he was slow. He endured patiently with sinners.

Not only was he patient with sinners, but he was patient with circumstances. He timed his miracles and his teachings so that his ministry would unfold according to the will of his Father. When prodded by his family to speed things up, he responded that his time had not yet come (John 2:1–5; 7:1–8). He knew how to wait patiently on the Lord.

He was also patient in suffering. The apostle Peter, eyewitness to the crucifixion, recalls the patience of Christ in affliction:

> For to this you have been called, because Christ also suffered for you, leaving you an example, so that you might follow in his steps. He committed no sin, neither was deceit found in his mouth. When he was reviled, he did not revile in return; when he suffered, he did not threaten, but continued entrusting himself to him who judges justly. He himself bore our sins in his body on the tree, that we might die to sin and live to righteousness. By his wounds you have been healed. (1 Pet. 2:21–24)

Patiently, he endured the cross. Christ is our example of patience with sinners, patience in circumstances, and patience in suffering. He shows us what perfect human patience looks like.

After making his famous declaration that he was the foremost among sinners, Paul mentions God's purpose in saving him: "But I received mercy for this reason, that in me, as the foremost, Jesus Christ might display his perfect patience as an example to those who were to believe in him for eternal life" (1 Tim. 1:16). Paul knew that the depth of his sin displayed the depth of Christ's patience. When we view our own salvation as an expression and example of the perfect patience of Christ, we begin to desire that our lives thereafter would exemplify that patience, as well. We begin to wait patiently on the Lord. We begin to bear patiently with others, even those who are the foremost among sinners.

Patient as He Is Patient

God's will for our lives is that we would be patient as he is patient. He wills that we would follow the example of Christ's patience and await the return of Christ patiently.

When we grow frustrated with a friend or family member who persists in sin, we can remember that Christ bears patiently with us. When we begin to think that a circumstance is stretching longer than we can take, we can remember the patience of Christ to wait on the Father's timing in all things. When we are weighed down by suffering, we can remember that in Christ's greatest moment of suffering he set his face like flint and even prayed for the forgiveness of his adversaries. And when we feel discouraged with ourselves for continuing to give in to sin, we can remind ourselves—and I can't believe I'm saying this—to be patient, because God isn't finished with us yet.

Nor is he finished with his church, his bride awaiting his return. Patience is not just the ability to wait, but to abide. It is not just gritting our teeth and waiting for a circumstance to change or a trial to resolve, crossing days off on a calendar. It is living daily in the awareness that God holds all things together, and that, in the grand scheme of things, whatever trouble we face during this life is light and momentary. Sin and suffering have an expiration date. They are not eternal. Those who wait patiently for the return of Christ do so with the assurance that all things will be made new and with the conviction that every day until that day counts toward eternity.

The church must be a bastion of patience. As the rest of the world chases the next new thing every eight seconds or less, we must be those who turn our eyes toward the long view. We must be known for our staying power when loving our neighbors takes longer than we expected and is harder than we thought. It takes patience to run with endurance, but that is the race the world needs to see us run. It may just be what catches and holds their attention in a goldfish world. Let patience be found among the people of God. He is not finished with us yet.

Verses for Meditation

Psalm 37:7
Psalm 86:15
Romans 15:4–5
Colossians 3:12–13
2 Peter 3:14–15

Questions for Reflection

1. Think of the person who is most likely to try your patience. What wrong expectations might be contributing your lack of patience with him or her? How does the example of Christ instruct you to reframe your expectations?

2. Reflect on Proverbs 19:11. How well does the term "slow to anger" describe you? What do you fear you will lose by choosing to overlook an offense?

3. How has a time of trial produced patience in you in a way you might not otherwise have developed it? What did you learn about God during that process? How did that experience change the way you understand the patience of Christ?

4. How have you known the patience of God as you have wrestled with ongoing sin in your own life? What does it look like to be patient with the sanctification process without excusing sin? Give an example.

Pray

Write a prayer to the Lord thanking him for his patience toward sinners, and toward you, in particular. Ask him to help you grow in patience with others, and to be better at waiting on him in your circumstances. Ask him to help you to be slow to anger and quick to overlook an offense. Thank him for the faithful example of Christ, who shows us the way of patience.

9

God Most Truthful

And though this world, with devils filled,
Should threaten to undo us,
We will not fear, for God has willed
His truth to triumph through us.

This morning before I sat down to write, I took some time to respond to emails. This is a classic pattern of procrastination for me on a writing day, intended to make me feel like I have at least accomplished reducing my inbox whether I manage to get any writing done or not. But today, my self-congratulatory process completely backfired.

In my inbox was an invitation to an event that I did not want to attend. The host, sensing that the RSVPs were coming in a little light, had asked all the invitees their reasons for not wanting to come. I crafted a response about how my family already had plans that weekend and how sorry I was to have to miss.

This was a lie. Please don't miss what I am saying: On the morning I set aside to write a chapter about the truthfulness of God, my first impulse on opening my computer was to misrepresent the truth. I deleted the response and sent one that, while still kindly and minimally worded, was at least honest. But I had to wonder if I would have acknowledged the prompting of my conscience had I not just spent several days researching the psychology of why we lie for this chapter. How many times do I shade the truth without hesitation, even without any real awareness that I am doing so?

Of all verbal skills, lying comes to us early and easily. Researchers even regard it as a sign of normal cognitive development when it first begins to emerge during toddlerhood.[1] Kind speech takes years to develop. Polite speech takes a thousand repetitions to ingrain in a child. But lying? It's as if we are born with the seeds of deceptiveness ready to sprout in us at the first signs of vocabulary.

Because, let's face it, that's exactly how we're born. Ever since the Father of Lies slithered into the garden and twisted the truth of the Father of Lights, humans have displayed an aptitude for speaking with the forked tongue of the Serpent. There we were, neatly tucked into Paradise, God's truth revealed to us as plain as day: Eat all you want from all these trees. Eat nothing from just this one, or you will die.

Enter the Liar, who in a smooth turn of phrase, did what liars do best. He questioned the credibility of the Truth-Giver, twisted his words, and then flatly denied his claims.

Not surprisingly, humanity wasted no time adopting the speech patterns of the one to whom they had succumbed. Adam's first recorded words after the fall are an untruth. When God asks where he is, Adam responds, "I heard the sound of you in the garden, and

I was afraid, because I was naked, and I hid myself" (Gen. 3:10). Of course, he is not afraid because he is naked. He is afraid because he has transgressed the law of God. When God asks him directly if he has eaten the forbidden fruit, Adam commits further to his deception by playing the victim: "The woman whom you gave to be with me, she gave me fruit of the tree, and I ate" (Gen. 3:12).

Wow, Adam. A simple "Yes" or "No" would suffice. No need to invent an excuse.

And in the midst of my eye-roll, I recall the matter of that RSVP I felt the need to embellish. Proverbs 12:22 says, "The LORD abhors a person who lies, but those who deal truthfully are his delight" (NET). Why such strong language directed at liars? Because those created in the image of Perfect Truth should reflect the absolute truthfulness of their Maker.

God Is Truth

God is truth. He is its origin and its determiner. What he defines as true is eternally true, unchangingly true. Because he is truth, all of his actions reveal truth and all of his words declare it. As the fullness of truth itself, God is incapable of lying, though sometimes our limited perception may cause us to doubt that this is the case. Satan knows this, and tempts us just as he tempted Eve. He suggests that if we sin, we will not surely die, as God has said. Like Eve, we cross the line into sin, only to find ourselves still breathing in and out—not dead—and we mistakenly assume that the Serpent is the bearer of truth. But time reveals that we are indeed surely dying—just as God has said. Sin is not merely the rejection of God's will. It is the rejection of truth, a denial of what is real (Rom. 1:25).

Not only does God tell the absolute truth about sin, he tells the absolute truth about grace. If we confess our sin and call upon the name of the Lord, he forgives, just as he has said. Though we were dead in our trespasses, he "made us alive together with Christ" (Eph. 2:5). Here also, Satan desires to make us question God's truthfulness. With every sin we commit as a Christian, we are tempted to fear that we have out-sinned God's grace. But just the fact that we are concerned about out-sinning God's grace is evidence that we are surely alive—just as God has said.

Truth is anything that conforms to reality. So, when we acknowledge God as truthful, we are doing more than affirming that he is honest. We are affirming that he defines reality. The temperature at which water boils is a reality. The height of Mount Kilimanjaro is a reality. These realities can be measured by humans. God defines those things. But our infinite God articulates a reality that goes beyond what humans are capable of measuring. We are notoriously bad at measuring the negative effects of sin, yet God is still faithful to point us to the truth of its killing capacity. We neglect to measure the positive effects of righteous living, yet God is still faithful to point us to the truth of its eternal value.

God, as the source and possessor of all knowledge, cannot be less than truthful. He defines reality because he is its origin. In making the claim that our God defines an objective reality, Christianity flatly denies the notion of moral relativism, that we decide what is right and wrong for ourselves. What God declares as good is truly good, and what God declares as bad is truly bad.

Truth with Trunk, Tusk, and Tail

Moral relativism, the idea that "what's right for you may not be right for me," is the product of finite minds. It is a way to accommodate the limited perspective that each of us necessarily operates from. Moral relativism asserts that personal truth is the highest form of truth we can possess, that no higher, absolute truth exists.

The classic illustration of this idea is the story of the blind men and the elephant. Depending on what part of the elephant he is touching, each perceives it to be an animal of a certain kind: one finds it to be like a wall, another like a serpent, another like a spear, and so on. We are to conclude from this illustration that it is possible for all the men to be correct, albeit partially so.

The story of the elephant finds its origins in Buddhist and Hindu writings. It assumes that all of us are blind. But what if there were a sighted person who could step in and edify the blind men as to the true nature of the elephant? Even better, what if that person were a miracle worker who could grant sight to the blind? Such a person might then just trouble himself further to assist those formerly blinded with how to properly perceive a world they had once navigated only in darkness. Now that would be a tale for the ages.

That would be the story of the Bible, the ultimate reality check for those wooed by moral relativism. The Bible declares that God himself is the benchmark for truth, the definer of reality, and that his creatures are subject to his definitions. Like the story of the elephant, it declares that people love darkness. But it also speaks of light coming into that darkness, resulting in the revelation of truth to those who were once blind. Like every belief system, Christianity asks and answers the existential questions all humans face:

- **Origin:** Where did I come from?
- **Purpose:** Why am I here?
- **Problem:** What's wrong?
- **Solution:** What fixes what's wrong?

The way the Bible answers these questions frames the Christian worldview, the reality from which we operate:

- **Origin:** We are not a cosmic accident; we were created by God.
- **Purpose:** We exist to bring glory to God and to enjoy him forever.
- **Problem:** Like Adam and Eve, we exchanged the truth of God for a lie and rebelled against our Creator, rendering us spiritually dead.
- **Solution:** God sent his Son to redeem us from death to life.

Sooner or later, every Christian will be called to defend this worldview. Most of us feel some level of panic at this thought. I am not a master of apologetics by any stretch, but the most compelling reason I have for believing the truthfulness of the Bible's claims is that it answers the questions of where we came from, why we are here, what is wrong, and what fixes what is wrong in a more compelling way than any other belief system I have encountered. The way it describes sin is accurate. The solution it proposes for sin transcends human effort. The purpose it gives for human existence, if embraced, causes people to live sacrificially.

The Christian worldview is a rational view. It is such because it is reality. It is not just rational; it is also good. God's truth is a good truth. Every other system of belief involves earning a reward through self-sacrifice or self-discipline. What is earned may be self-awareness or paradise, depending on the belief system in view, but only Christianity casts off the notion of earning. Only Christianity proposes a permanent solution to the burden of our guilt. Only Christianity speaks of the life of self-sacrifice as the end rather than the means, as the grateful response rather than the grit-your-teeth remedy. God's reality is true, and God's reality is good.

Shared Truth

The Bible contradicts not only moral relativism, but it also contradicts any notion of a personal truth that exists independent of shared truth. God's truth is communal, given not merely so that the individual can live in right relationship to God, but so that the individual can live in right relationship with others. The Christian faith holds no room for individualism. No sooner is Adam created than God declares his aloneness "not good" and remedies the situation with community. The believer, though called to a personal relationship with God, is simultaneously called to a communal relationship with other believers. Christian belief and isolationism are antithetical ideas.

Currently, the prevailing cultural message is "live your truth." I do not mean to imply that culture has hatched a new darling idea. It has just labeled the same old, nothing-new-under-the-sun self-worshiping individualism with an updated turn of phrase. "Follow your heart," "If it feels good, do it," or even the words of Pilate to Jesus, "What is truth?" are all ways of saying that truth is in the eye of the beholder. You could substitute any of those phrases in place of the Serpent's "You will not surely die," and the story of the fall would be unaltered.

Problematically, since the garden, sin has felt more normal to us than righteousness. To "live my truth" is to live in what feels normal to me, to walk in the way that seems right unto man (Prov. 14:12). The problem with living my truth is that, above all else, the heart is deceitful and desperately wicked (Jer. 17:9). It creates a false reality for me based on my natural preferences, a reality in which my preferences and desires tend to take precedence over those of others. Living my truth will inevitably prevent someone else from living theirs if our preferences are at odds with one another. Living my truth destroys my ability to live in community as I was intended, a community predicated not on actualizing all of my personal preferences, but on laying them down for the good of others. The problem with living my truth is that my truth is a lie.

Instead of "living my truth," may God direct me into living his, the only one there really is—the truth that rejects isolation instead of creating it. To do so is to plunge myself into the community that only a shared truth preserves.

Fresh Words

In recent years, the church has emphasized the personal nature of the gospel, a distinguishing and truly beautiful mark of our faith. However, inadvertently, the corporate nature of the gospel has sometimes fallen from view. Our worship services often follow suit. Our church websites might state creeds we align with and liturgies we confess, but fewer and fewer churches recite them as a church body. Corporate confession falls to the wayside as we plan our time as a church body with a focus on the experience of the individual over the expression of the community. This mind-set runs the risk of echoing the secular notion that truth is mine to do with as I please.

We need our gathering times to remind us that the truth we are staking our lives on is a truth we share with every believer in our congregation. Moreover, it is a truth we share with every believer who has ever lived. It is an ancient truth that suffers no loss of integrity with the passage of time. In fact, the longer it endures, the more its witness is confirmed.

Every word of God is true and good, but not only that, none of them ever grow stale. The practice of asking God for a "fresh word," a new truth personalized for us, has grown more and more popular. I don't think any of us would argue that we have adored and adhered to the ancient words thoroughly enough that a request for new ones could be credible. Faced with uncertainty or difficulty, or just spiritual malaise, my perception is that it would *feel* better if the words were meant strictly for me and my circumstance. But it is not new truths we need; we need old truths recently forgotten. It is not personal truths we need, but rather shared truth preserved and passed down from one believing generation to the next, personalized to us in our current day. That shared truth is available within the pages of God's Word to me and to all who believe.

Jesus tells his disciples, "If you abide in my word, you are truly my disciples, and you will know the truth, and the truth will set you free" (John 8:31–32). Jesus's call is to abide in what has already been given, what's been passed down to us. By abiding in the word of Jesus, we will know what is truth and thereby be set free from error. Not only that, but we will be set free from our deceitful hearts, receiving "truth in the inward being" (Ps. 51:6).

Inspired by the Holy Spirit, the writers of Scripture wrote with an intended meaning in view. Time and culture may separate us from that meaning, but our task is to find the timeless, culture-transcending, shared application of that text by unearthing its intended meaning. Regarding the Bible as shared truth helps us avoid the pitfall of becoming consumed with "what this verse means to me" in our study of it. Our task is not to assign a personal meaning to the text. The text will yield a personal application, but it will flow from and submit to the objective, careful, contextualized interpretation of the author's meaning. "What this verse means to me" can only be considered after "what this verse means" has been given our full consideration.

Even as those with spiritual eyes to recognize truth, we

are sometimes selective in the truths we gaze upon. We can become too fixated on one part of the elephant, loving one part to the detriment of the whole. The believer is charged to seek and observe the truth, the whole truth, and nothing but the truth. The full counsel of God's Word is necessary to fulfilling this charge.

Know the Truth

In the art world, fraudulent paintings represent a risk for art dealers and customers. Knowing how to spot a fake is important. The same is true of counterfeit money. Even in the age of e-commerce, counterfeit money remains a problem of costly proportions. The Federal Reserve Bank of Chicago estimates that over $61 million in fake currency is currently in circulation in the United States.[2] Counterfeiters rely on our inability to distinguish the difference between real and fake paintings or bills. Fraud investigators can't learn to spot a fake by studying only counterfeits. The best weapon they have in detecting fraud is knowledge of the original. They learn to discern what is fake by studying what is real.

The same is true of Jesus's disciples. We can't discern what's false if we don't train our eyes on what is true. The best weapon we have for discerning true teaching from false teaching and sin from righteousness is "the sword of the spirit, the Word of God" (Eph. 6:17). The Word of God is a weapon, forged to combat forgery. We must know how to handle the Bible rightly, and we must know it as comprehensibly as possible in our lifetime. If spiritual warfare is the purview of the Father of Lies, we must arm ourselves with truth. Truth is a book, and that book is a weapon.

Truth is also a person.

Jesus Christ, the Word made flesh, embodies truth for us.

He declares himself "the way, and the truth, and the life" (John 14:6). He shows us what truth, rightly handled, looks like. With it, he rebukes the Pharisee and woos the wayward. With it, he cuts through the lies of Satan in the wilderness. With it, he instructs his disciples and corrects the false teaching of his day. The Word of Truth utters, "Truly, truly, I say to you . . ." and blessed are all who respond with the amen.

He is ascended into heaven, but we remain. We are now the embodiment of truth, the keepers of reality, "the church of the living God, a pillar and buttress of the truth" (1 Tim. 3:15). What is the will of God for your life? His will is that you know the truth (John 8:32). That you walk in the truth (3 John 1:4). That you speak the truth in love (Eph. 4:15). That you be sanctified in truth (John 17:17). That you rejoice in the truth (1 Cor. 13:6). That you rightly handle the truth (2 Tim. 2:15). That you obey the truth (1 Pet. 1:22).

God's will is that you take your place among the community of believers as a truth-bearer in a world full of lies. Honesty should characterize all of your dealings, great and small, so that when you are asked to give a reason for what you believe, your credibility is a foregone conclusion. And when you are asked, proclaim Christ as the way, the truth, and the life. Invite them to what is real.

Verses for Meditation

Numbers 23:19
Psalm 19:9
Psalm 119:160
Isaiah 45:19
John 1:14
John 8:31–32
John 17:17–19

Questions for Reflection

1. How prone are you to lying or shading the truth? In what situations are you most likely to lie? What are you trying to protect or escape when you do so?

2. How has moral relativism ("what's right for you may not be right for me") shaped your own thinking? What underlying motives drive us to want to embrace moral relativism?

3. How does confession of sin relate to being a person who walks in the truth? What does an unwillingness or slowness to confess sin indicate about how much we value truthfulness?

4. How should a desire to grow in truthfulness impact our relationship with God positively? How should it impact our relationships with others positively? Give a specific example of each.

Pray

Write a prayer to God asking him to write his truth in your inward being. Ask him to build in you a hatred for dishonesty, a discernment for false teaching, and a love for the truth of his Word. Thank him for the freedom you have received through Jesus Christ, the very Truth of God.

10

God Most Wise

To God the only wise,
Our Savior and our King,
Let all the saints below the skies
Their humble praises bring.

On October 2, 1950, wisdom quietly announced itself in four hand-drawn black-and-white frames in, of all places, the comic strip section of the newspaper. On that day, the world was introduced to Charlie Brown, the awkward and lovable centerpiece of a group of children (and a dog and a bird) who would charm readers for fifty years as the Peanuts gang.[1] At the height of its popularity, Charles Schulz's beloved comic strip ran in more than 2,600 newspapers, reaching 355 million readers in 75 countries.[2]

What was the secret to its success? No doubt, the relatable struggles the characters faced and the humor Schultz drew from them appealed to us, but an additional piece of writing genius was at work: Schultz's children spoke with wisdom beyond their years:

"I've developed a new philosophy. I only dread one day at a time!" —Charlie Brown

"Life is like a ten-speed bicycle . . . some of us have gears we never use." —Linus van Pelt

"It's just human nature . . . we all need someone to kiss us goodbye." —Marcie Johnson[3]

In books and movies, we adore the trope of the wise child. C. S. Lewis and J. K. Rowling have demonstrated the lasting power and appeal of such characters. The idea is intriguing to us because intuitively, we associate wisdom with age and maturity. Deep wisdom is not the norm among children—it is most often the product of years of learning and experience. When looking for a mentor, no one goes to a preschool.

Job reflects, "Wisdom is with the aged, and understanding in length of days" (Job 12:12). Think, then, how much wisdom resides in the One who is called the Ancient of Days.

Wisdom is closely related to knowledge, but distinct from it. Knowledge is possessing the facts. Wisdom is the ability to achieve the best ends with the facts. Wisdom is the ability to make good decisions based on the knowledge available. The wisest human you know is capable of choosing wrongly, simply because he does not possess all the facts. Wise humans choose wisely by taking the facts they know and extrapolating the best course of action.

Because God is not bound by time, he is able to determine the end from the beginning, acting within time with perfect awareness of all outcomes. Think, then, how much wisdom resides in the One who holds all knowledge. Because God holds all knowledge, he is able to choose perfect ends.

God, by contrast to you and me, never extrapolates.

Possessing all the facts, he combines them with perfect insight, and chooses wisely every time. Wise humans may have their judgment clouded by personal bias, but God is free of that limit as well. His wisdom is perfect. It is also implicitly good. We may speak of a malevolent person as an "evil genius," but we do not credit wisdom to him. Wisdom implies moral goodness, which God possesses in infinite supply. The paths he chooses are always wise and always good.

Though wisdom is a sign of maturity in humans, it is a simple fact in God. He does not grow in wisdom—he is infinitely wise and his wisdom never waxes or wanes. God understands everything exactly the right way and does everything exactly the right way. He always has, and he always will. His wisdom transcends human wisdom by an infinite distance: "For the foolishness of God is wiser than human wisdom, and the weakness of God is stronger than human strength" (1 Cor. 1:25 NIV).

Wisdom and Folly

Given our relatively limited ability to obtain and retain knowledge, it is amazing that any of us ever receive the designation of "wise." But remarkably, humans can learn to operate in wisdom if they so choose. Though wisdom is associated with maturity, it is not a guaranteed gift of the aging process. It is possible to live a life of folly from start to finish.

Because we are designed to live in community with others, a life spent in folly always affects more than just the individual who chooses it. Wisdom is desirable among humans because, in choosing the best outcomes, we look to serve the greater good, not just ourselves. Wisdom aids community. It allows us to live at peace with one another. Folly seeks to serve self alone and pulls the community into chaos.

Folly is the "way that seems right to a man" (Prov. 14:12). With our usual flair for the upside down, we call wise what is foolish and foolish what is wise. The apostle Paul warned the church at Corinth regarding the tendency to call folly wisdom:

> Let no one deceive himself. If anyone among you thinks that he is wise in this age, let him become a fool that he may become wise. For the wisdom of this world is folly with God. For it is written, "He catches the wise in their craftiness," and again, "The Lord knows the thoughts of the wise, that they are futile." (1 Cor. 3:18–20)

We love to deceive ourselves that in choosing self, we have chosen rightly. And we love to deceive others that our choosing of self is actually not selfish. We become wise in our own eyes, as Proverbs says, giving the appearance of wisdom, but inwardly desiring the approval of others.

When the Bible makes the distinction between Godly wisdom and worldly wisdom, it is not separating a higher form of wisdom from a lesser one; it is distinguishing between true and false, between wisdom and folly. Worldly wisdom is not wisdom at all. James writes:

> Who is wise and understanding among you? By his good conduct let him show his works in the meekness of wisdom. But if you have bitter jealousy and selfish ambition in your hearts, do not boast and be false to the truth. This is not the wisdom that comes down from above, but is earthly, unspiritual, demonic. For where jealousy and selfish ambition exist, there will be disorder and every vile practice. But the wisdom from above is first pure, then peaceable, gentle, open to reason, full of mercy and good fruits, impartial and sincere. And a harvest of

righteousness is sown in peace by those who make peace. (James 3:13–18)

Note the sharp contrast James makes. Worldly wisdom and Godly wisdom are antithetical and adversarial:

Worldly wisdom self-promotes. Godly wisdom elevates others.
Worldly wisdom seeks the highest place. Godly wisdom seeks the lowest place.
Worldly wisdom avoids the mirror of the Word. Godly wisdom submits to the mirror of the Word.
Worldly wisdom trusts in earthly possessions. Godly wisdom trusts in treasures in heaven.
Worldly wisdom boasts. Godly wisdom is slow to speak.
Worldly wisdom says trials will crush you. Godly wisdom says trials will mature you.
Worldly wisdom says temptation is no big deal. Godly wisdom says temptation indulged leads to death.
Worldly wisdom says, "Seeing is believing." Godly wisdom says, "Blessed are those who have not seen and yet have believed" (John 20:29).
Worldly wisdom wields might. Godly wisdom works in meekness.

Simply put, any thought, word, or deed that compromises our ability to love God and neighbor is folly. Utter foolishness. The height of stupidity. The worldly-wise place themselves in opposition to God, operating from their own perspective of what is best, a perspective that seeks only the best for them.

But the same writer who implores us to distinguish and avoid worldly wisdom is also eager for us to know how to possess Godly wisdom. James reminds us that it is ours for the asking: "If any of you lacks wisdom, let him ask God, who gives generously to all without reproach, and it will be given him" (James 1:5). This is a stupendous statement. Lack wisdom? Just ask. God will give it. Period.

If you find you lack insight and understanding, consider the possibility that you do not have because you do not ask. God waits for your request, eager to grant it.

Asking for Wisdom

In 1 Kings 3, we find King Solomon doing exactly what James instructs. He is probably in his early twenties, ascending the throne to take his seat after the most celebrated king of Israel, his father, David. It's hard enough to rule a great nation, but even harder to do so in the shadow of your legendary father. God tells Solomon he will grant whatever request he asks. Faced with the classic genie-in-the-lamp scenario, Solomon asks not for riches or power, but for wisdom to discern good from evil so that he can govern wisely. And God grants it. Immediately, Solomon finds himself in a very public trial of his abilities to govern. With the eyes of a nation upon him, he hears two women plead their case against each other.

They are prostitutes, living in the same house, both recent mothers of baby sons. It's remarkable that their case is heard at all, as they inhabit the very bottom of the social ladder. Already, Solomon has demonstrated the wisdom of compassion and non-favoritism just by hearing them. But greater wisdom still will be required to administer justice. One of the babies has died, and the women dispute over whose is the living child. It is one woman's word against the other's. There are no security cameras or eyewitnesses to bring testimony; there are no DNA tests to establish parentage. There is only Solomon, bearing the scrutiny of a sea of staring eyes, awaiting how he will rule.

This is the point where we would act differently—more spiritually, if you will—than Solomon does. Faced with a seemingly unsolvable situation, we would ask everyone for a brief moment in which to seek the Lord. We would bow our heads piously and pray: "Lord, you know all things. You desire justice. Please tell me the identity of the rightful mother." What could be wrong with that prayer? It is an honest plea for wisdom in a hard situation, isn't it?

Yet, that is not what Solomon does at all. Instead, in one of the most dramatic scenes in all of Scripture, Solomon commands, "Bring me a sword. . . . Divide the living child in two, and give half to the one and half to the other" (1 Kings 3:24–25). Immediately, the real mother pleads that the baby be spared and given to her adversary. Her identity revealed, her child is restored to her, "and all Israel heard of the judgment that the king had rendered, and they stood in awe of the king, because they perceived that the wisdom of God was in him to do justice" (1 Kings 3:28).

Wisdom Versus Knowledge

I like so many things about this story. I like that even the least in Israel receives justice and compassion instead of "case dismissed." I like that a good mother receives back her child. I like that a young leader receives encouragement and affirmation. But I also like how this story clarifies for us what it means to act in wisdom.

Faced with a similar situation, you and I would pray what we would call a prayer for wisdom, when, in fact, it is a prayer for knowledge. We often confuse the two. Solomon, who knows he has already received wisdom from God, does not ask God for knowledge. He already possesses all the knowledge he needs to act wisely. Solomon takes what he knows about human nature, about a woman's natural desire to protect her child, and he uses it to expose the true motives of the women. And God honors the faith he displays in that process.

Often, we pray for wisdom when, in fact, we are seeking knowledge. Tell me what to do, Lord. Tell me which commitment to accept, what words to say, where to live, and who to work for. We may even remind God that in James 1:5 he told us we would receive wisdom if we asked. But we are not asking for understanding; we are asking for information. And in doing so, we betray our unwillingness to move from immaturity to maturity as a disciple.

My daughter Mary Kate is home from college for the summer. She is twenty years old. Imagine if she came into the kitchen on a June morning in Texas and asked me, "Mom, what should I wear today, a T-shirt or a sweater?" "Mom, what should I have for breakfast?" "Mom, which shoes should I wear?" At her age, these questions would be inappropriate, maybe even cause for concern. My job as a parent is to raise my child to have an internal framework for making decisions. I shouldn't be spoon-feeding her information at age twenty.

How much more so our heavenly parent? Having granted Solomon an internal framework for making decisions, Solomon does not ask for knowledge in the moment of the decision point. He uses the knowledge he has to make the best decision he can. Wisdom is a mark of spiritual maturity. The author of Hebrews notes this connection:

> For though by this time you ought to be teachers, you need someone to teach you again the basic principles of the oracles of God. You need milk, not solid food, for everyone who lives on milk is unskilled in the word of righteousness, since he is a child. But solid food is for the mature, for those who have their powers of discernment trained by constant practice to distinguish good from evil. (Heb. 5:12–14)

The spiritually mature develop the ability to discern what is good and what is evil. They move beyond being told basic truths to internalizing them so they perceive the world differently. They are transformed by the renewing of their minds, "that by testing [they] may discern what is the will of God, what is good and acceptable and perfect" (Rom. 12:2).

I wish that the rest of Solomon's story had followed the course of his early years. Later in his life, he wandered from the path of Godly wisdom onto the path of folly. The man who wrote that "the fear of the LORD is the beginning of wisdom" (Prov. 9:10) traded the fear of the Lord for the fear of man, thereby trading wisdom for folly. He devoted himself to sensuality, wealth, and power. His story teaches us that there is no such thing as "once wise, always wise" for anyone but God. Like patience, mercy, and grace, we must remain constantly aware of our need for a sustaining supply of wisdom.

Keep Asking

In the Sermon on the Mount, Jesus tells his disciples to "ask, and it will be given to you; seek, and you will find; knock, and it will be opened to you. For everyone who asks receives, and the one who seeks finds, and to the one who knocks it will be opened" (Matt. 7:7–8). We read these words and begin to make a list of the information or the possessions we would like to get from God. But I believe Jesus has a better request list in mind when he speaks these instructions. Jesus's disciples, overwhelmed with the cost of following him, would not have heard his statement as an invitation to request new fishing boats or bigger houses. They would have heard them as an invitation to request spiritual resources—patience, courage, compassion, perhaps—or wisdom. Not accidentally, Jesus's directive to ask sounds very close to that of his half-brother James regarding asking for wisdom.

The verb tense for *ask*, *seek*, and *knock* communicates not a one-time request but an ongoing one: *keep on* asking, *keep on* seeking, *keep on* knocking. For those who understand the sorrow and destruction of a life of folly, no prayer request will be more urgent or more ongoing than the one for wisdom.

If any of you lacks wisdom, let him *keep on* asking God.

But how does God give wisdom? How can we hope to develop this inner sense of discernment between good and evil? We do so by declaring as Solomon did, "Bring me a sword": "For the word of God is living and active, sharper than any two-edged sword, piercing to the division of soul and of spirit, of joints and of marrow, and discerning the thoughts and intentions of the heart" (Heb. 4:12).

The Word of God gives us discernment into what is arguably the area we need it most: the thoughts and intentions of our own hearts. In seeing our own depravity, we develop a right reverence (fear) of the Lord. And wisdom begins to be formed in us. When God points out your sin, you are wise to turn from it. The most basic act of wisdom is repentance. Turning from sin trains us in how to hate it, in how to anticipate the temptation points, and in how to seek the Holy Spirit's aid in finding the way of escape.

It is not coincidental that a lack of discernment and a neglected Bible are so often found in company. The Bible contains for us ancient words of wisdom, and it tells us also of the example of Christ, who became for us wisdom from God:

> For you see your calling, brethren, that not many wise according to the flesh, not many mighty, not many noble, are called. But God has chosen the foolish things of the world to put to shame the wise, and God has chosen the weak things

of the world to put to shame the things which are mighty . . .
that no flesh should glory in His presence. But of Him you
are in Christ Jesus, who became for us wisdom from God—
and righteousness and sanctification and redemption—that,
as it is written, "He who glories, let him glory in the Lord."
(1 Cor. 1:26–31 NKJV)

If any of you is weak, if any of you is foolish, if any of you
has gloried in lesser things, turn your eyes upon Christ Jesus,
who became for us wisdom from God.

Solomon stopped asking. May the same never be said of us.

What is the will of God for your life? If any of you lack
wisdom, ask.

Verses for Meditation
Job 12:13–17
Job 36:5
Psalm 147:5
Proverbs 2:6
Isaiah 55:8–9
Daniel 2:20
Romans 11:33
Romans 16:25–27

Questions for Reflection
1. If God told you he would give you anything you wanted, would
   wisdom be the first thing you would request? How would receiving wisdom alter the current list of requests you are placing
   before the Lord?

2. Think of your greatest moment (or season) of foolishness. How has God used that experience to grow wisdom in you as you have matured in your faith? What did he teach you?

3. Think of the wisest person you have ever known. How did that person model the wisdom of God for you? How did his or her example teach you to discern good from evil?

4. How should a desire to grow in wisdom impact our relationship with God positively? How should it impact our relationships with others positively? Give a specific example of each.

Pray

Write a prayer to God asking him to show you where worldly wisdom has governed your thoughts, words, and actions. Ask him to show you where you have requested knowledge instead of discernment. Ask him not only to grant you wisdom but to prompt you to *keep on asking* for wisdom. Praise him that he reveals wisdom to us in his Word and in the example of Christ. Thank him that he gives wisdom for the asking.

Conclusion

Engraved with His Image

Render to Caesar the things that are Caesar's, and
to God the things that are God's.

Mark 12:17

In the opening lines of this book, I asked you to consider that
the hope of the gospel in our sanctification is not simply that we
would make better choices, but that we would *become better
people*. By asking the better question of "Who should I be?" we
find that the will of God for our lives is not hidden. The Bible
is filled with exhortations for how we can reflect our Creator as
we become increasingly like Christ.

But in suggesting that we are to become better people, how
do we avoid succumbing to something resembling a Christian-
ized self-help program? How do we keep from slipping into a
mind-set that accomplishes nothing more than behavior modification? Make no mistake, the Bible teaches us that behavior
modification should absolutely follow salvation. But it occurs
for a different reason than it does in the life of the unbeliever.

There is a difference between self-help and sanctification, and that difference is the motive of the heart.[1]

We seek to be holy as God is holy as a joyful act of gratitude. We never seek holiness as a means to earn God's favor or to avoid his displeasure. We have his favor, and his pleasure rests upon us. The motive of sanctification is joy.

Joy is both our motive and our reward. Jesus made this connection for his disciples: "If you keep my commandments, you will abide in my love, just as I have kept my Father's commandments and abide in his love. These things I have spoken to you, that my joy may be in you, and that your joy may be full" (John 15:10–11).

Fullness of joy results when we seek to reflect our Maker. It is what we were created to do. It is the very will of God for our lives.

In elementary school, I shared an interest in coin collecting with my two older brothers. We assembled a modest collection of coins—a Mercury dime, some wheat pennies, an Eisenhower silver dollar, and a Morgan silver dollar from 1900 discovered forgotten in the keepsake box of an ancient family member now deceased. We were enormously proud of our coins. We kept them enshrined in a large, flat display box of cardboard with a glass lid. Little did we know the glass lid would prove more valuable than the coin collection itself.

The front door of our house contained a circular window at eye level, which was covered on the inside by a small, sheer curtain. One day while our mother was at work, we accidentally broke that window. I'll leave you to speculate on the circumstances surrounding the accident, but you should assume mischief was a factor. Fearing our mother's just displeasure, we united in a rare act of sibling solidarity: Conceal the crime and fix the window. We pooled our finances and scheduled the repair, but there would be a three-day wait before the glass could be replaced. We panicked. Three sweltering Texas summer days is too long to conceal a broken window, and Mom would be home from work soon. In a stroke of miscreant genius, we duct-taped that glass lid from the coin collection across the window, concealed behind the curtain. Mom never found out.

As a parent, now when I think of coin collecting, my first thought is never to leave my children at home unsupervised. But my second thought—as a Bible teacher—is of a story recorded for us in the Gospel of Mark.

A Story That Is Not about Taxes

In Mark 12, Jesus is asked a question regarding the paying of taxes. Two adversarial groups of Jews, the Herodians and the Pharisees, try to trap Jesus into saying that Rome is their rightful ruler. The Romans employed Jewish tax collectors to extract taxes (often unfairly) from their own people. Jesus's disciple Matthew was one such tax collector before his conversion. The subject of paying taxes to Rome was a highly flammable one, and if his enemies could get Jesus to speak in support of the system, they could easily raise a rabble against him.

With smooth talk, his Jewish adversaries pose their question: Is it lawful to pay taxes to Caesar or not? Jesus knows the question is a trap, so he responds in his typical fashion: he uses their question to answer a more important one, one that addresses not outward actions but inward motives. He asks them to bring him a denarius, the coin used to pay the tax. He then poses a question to them that is its own sort of trap:

> They brought the coin, and he asked them, "Whose image is this? And whose inscription?"

"Caesar's," they replied.

Then Jesus said to them, "Give back to Caesar what is Caesar's and to God what is God's."

And they were amazed at him. (Mark 12:16–17 NIV)

We read this story and can tell that something in Jesus's response has derailed their entrapment in a way that leaves them amazed, and a little trapped themselves, though it is not immediately clear to our modern ears how he has done so. But a little insight from the average coin collector can help us piece together what transpired.

The coin shown to Jesus is most likely a denarius of the Emperor Tiberius. Two thousand years later, these coins still exist. You could purchase one right now on eBay for about eight hundred dollars. Coins minted during the reign of a particular emperor were stamped with a picture of his face and an inscription. The inscription circling the face of Tiberius reads, "Caesar Augustus Tiberius, son of the Divine Augustus," reinforcing the common claim that the Caesars themselves were gods. Tiberius's father, Augustus, had been worshiped as a god throughout the Roman Empire during his lifetime, and the inscription attempts to elevate Tiberius to the same status.

When Jesus responds to his adversaries, he doesn't really talk about taxes at all. Instead he talks about the coin itself; he talks about image bearing. He says, in effect, "The coin is engraved with the image of a 'god,' marking what belongs to him. You, on the other hand, are engraved with the image of God himself, marking what belongs to him. Will you concern yourself with earthly obligations to the neglect of the heavenly ones required by the image engraved in you?

"You bear the very marks of the Creator. Render unto God what is God's."

The Jewish leaders of Jesus's day showed more concern for who ruled earthly kingdoms than for who ruled the kingdom of heaven. In the process, they rendered service to false gods. We can be guilty of doing the same. We are always looking to fashion an idol.

Inadequate Idols

When God gives the Law to Moses at Mount Sinai, he gives a set of ten commandments. Eight of them are briefly stated, but two of them are expressed at some length. The longest is the fourth command, to remember the Sabbath and keep it holy. The next longest, only slightly shorter in length, is the second command:

> You shall not make for yourself a carved image, or any likeness of anything that is in heaven above, or that is in the earth beneath, or that is in the water under the earth. You shall not bow down to them or serve them, for I the LORD your God am a jealous God, visiting the iniquity of the fathers on the children to the third and the fourth generation of those who hate me, but showing steadfast love to thousands of those who love me and keep my commandments. (Ex. 20:4–6)

Though only the fourth command explicitly states the idea of remembering, the extended length of both the fourth and the second command points to the idea in both. When I wanted my small children to follow instructions, I always devoted more explanation to the parts that were the least likely to be remembered, understood, or obeyed. So also, God gives extra words where extra emphasis is needed.

We need an extra-firm reminder about the second command concerning idols. In one sense, it is an extension of the first command to have no other gods before God, but it carries more specificity.

The term "carved image" is variously translated "image," "graven image," or "idol." We read the second command and recognize that God does not want us to take inanimate materials and form them into an image that we then worship. Simple enough, we think, trying hard not to notice how closely our phones, our cars, or our bank statements resemble that description.

But there's a grander significance to why God says not to make graven images. He himself has already done so: "Then God said, 'Let us make humankind in our image, after our likeness'" (Gen. 1:26 NET).

In all of the created order, only humans are designed to reflect the image of God. To form a likeness of an animal or a human, or even of God himself, from wood or metal or clay could only at best be a shadow of a shadow of a reality. At worst, it's a lie. God forbids the making of graven images on the grounds that he has already engraved his image on us.

What can be known of God from humans formed in his image is incomplete and marred by the fall. But what if one were born who could restore that image to what it should have been? Here another coin-collecting insight can help us with a modern-day analogy.

God's Will, a Flawless Impression

The United States Mint creates proof sets for coins, which are highly collectible because they are the most flawless version of a particular coin to be found. Proofs are often cast in gold, silver, or platinum, rather than the lesser metal of the actual coin that is in circulation. They are an idealized version of what we carry in our pockets, unsullied by the everyday wear and tear of commerce.

Jesus Christ is the living proof of God, the perfect image bearer, pure and imminently valuable, unsullied by sin.

Because of the fall, you and I are heavily circulated, dinged-up, base-metal fodder for the parking meter. But we still bear the image of our God, if only faintly. When we joyfully embrace the call to be holy as he is holy, those worn-down contours of his likeness begin to be restored to sharpness. The divots and scratches inflicted by the fall and by our own folly begin to be erased. As we grow in holiness, love, goodness, justice, mercy, grace, faith, patience, truth, and wisdom, we look increasingly like Christ, who looks exactly like God.

Becoming better people is the process of reflecting with increasing clarity and fidelity the very face of God. God's will for our lives is that we be restored to mint condition. God's will for our lives is that we become living proof.

Everything we say or do will either illuminate or obscure the character of God. Sanctification is the process of joyfully growing luminous. Through Christ and by the Spirit, we have regained access to God's presence. And the result is the glorious reclamation of the image of God in man.

"And we all, with unveiled face, beholding the glory of the Lord, are being transformed into the same image from one degree of glory to another. For this comes from the Lord who is the Spirit" (2 Cor. 3:18).

Notes

Chapter 1: God Most Holy

1. See my *None Like Him* (Wheaton, IL: Crossway, 2016), 16.
2. Wilkin, *None Like Him*.
3. This thought is adapted from the opening lines of A. W. Tozer's classic book, *The Knowledge of the Holy*: "What comes into our minds when we think about God is the most important thing about us" (San Francisco: HarperCollins, 1992), 1.
4. Arthur Walkington Pink, *The Attributes of God* (Grand Rapids, MI: Baker, 1996), 41.
5. R. C. Sproul, *The Holiness of God* (Wheaton, IL: Tyndale, 2006), 25.
6. Jerry Bridges, *The Pursuit of Holiness* (Colorado Springs: NavPress, 2016), 21.

Chapter 2: God Most Loving

1. "Romantic Drama 1980-present," Box Office Mojo, accessed June 26, 2017, http://www.boxofficemojo.com/genres/chart/?id=romantic drama.htm.
2. Marcus Moore, "Couple Celebrates 75th Wedding Anniversary," WFAA.com, March 17, 2016, http://www.wfaa.com/features/couple -celebrates-75th-wedding-anniversary/31561702.
3. Though they have been widely explored, perhaps the best-known discussion of these ideas is C. S. Lewis's *The Four Loves*.
4. As with the English language, the same word can be used differently depending on the context. In some contexts, *phileo* and *agape* are used interchangeably (as in John 21:15–17). Though a count of a particular word usage may give some insight into the message of the New Testament, the theme of unconditional and active love expressed by God

toward the believer, and by the believer toward others, is undeniably pervasive.

5. Kenneth Wuest, *Wuest's Word Studies in the Greek New Testament* (Grand Rapids, MI: Eerdmans, 1975), 3:111–13.

Chapter 3: God Most Good

1. Alexandra Larkin, "Boy Finds Huge 7.44 Carat Diamond in State Park," CNN.com, March 16, 2017, http://www.cnn.com/2017/03/16 /us/arkansas-boy-diamond-trnd/.
2. Karl Zinsmeister, "Oseola McCarty," The Philanthropy Roundtable, "The Philanthropy Hall of Fame," accessed June 27, 2017, http://www .philanthropyroundtable.org/almanac/hall_of_fame/oseola_mccarty/.
3. Rick Bragg, "All She Has, $150,000, Is Going to a University," *The New York Times* online, August 12, 1995, http://www.nytimes.com /1995/08/13/us/all-she-has-150000-is-going-to-a-university.html.

Chapter 5: God Most Merciful

1. A. W. Tozer, *Knowledge of the Holy: The Attributes of God* (San Francisco: HarperCollins, 1992), 140.
2. James Montgomery Boice, *The Parables of Jesus* (Chicago: Moody Press, 1983), 89–91.
3. Boice, *Parables of Jesus*, 182.

Chapter 6: God Most Gracious

1. A. W. Tozer, *Knowledge of the Holy: The Attributes of God* (San Francisco: HarperCollins, 1992), 148–49.
2. Dietrich Bonhoeffer, *The Cost of Discipleship* (New York: Touchstone, 1995), 43–44.
3. D. A. Carson, *For the Love of God: A Daily Companion for Discovering the Riches of God's Word* (Wheaton, IL: Crossway, 2006), 23.

Chapter 7: God Most Faithful

1. Nathaniel P. Langford, "The Wonders of the Yellowstone," *Scribner's Monthly* 2, no. 1 (May 1871): 123.

Chapter 8: God Most Patient

1. Christopher Muther, "Instant Gratification Is Making Us Perpetually Impatient," *The Boston Globe* online, February 2, 2013.
2. John Stevens, "Decreasing Attention Spans and Your Website, Social Media Strategy," *Adweek* online, June 7, 2016, http://www.adweek.com /digital/john-stevens-guest-post-decreasing-attention-spans/.

Chapter 9: God Most Truthful

1. Yudhijit Bhattacharjee, "Why We Lie: The Science Behind Our Deceptive Ways," *National Geographic* online, June 15, 2017, https://www.national geographic.com/magazine/2017/06/lying-hoax-false-fibs-science/.
2. Geoff Williams, "In the Age of Digital Money, Counterfeit Bills Still a Problem," *U.S. News and World Report* online, April 25, 2013, https://money.usnews.com/money/personal-finance/articles/2013/04/25/how -to-spot-counterfeit-money.

Chapter 10: God Most Wise

1. Katherine Brooks, "10 of the Best Snoopy Moments to Celebrate 'Peanuts' 63rd Anniversary," *Huffpost*, October 2, 2013, https://www .huffingtonpost.com/2013/10/02/peanuts-anniversary_n_4025927.html/.
2. Pamela J. Podger, "Saying Goodbye: Friends and Family Eulogize Cartoonist Charles Schulz," *SFGATE*, February 22, 2000, http://www .sfgate.com/bayarea/article/SAYING-GOODBYE-Friends-and-family -eulogize-2774210.php/.
3. Reader's Digest Editors, "10 Great Quotes from the 'Peanuts' Comic Strip," *Reader's Digest* online, April 3, 2017, https://www.rd.com/culture /peanuts-quotes/.

Conclusion

1. Jen Wilkin, "Failure Is Not a Virtue," The Gospel Coalition website, May 1, 2014, https://www.thegospelcoalition.org/article/failure-is-not -a-virtue/.

General Index

Scripture Index

Go Deeper in Your Study of God and His Word

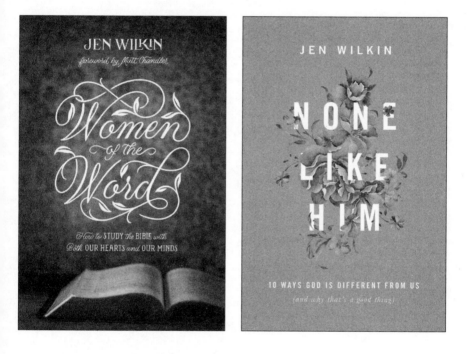

Personal Reflections

Personal Reflections

Personal Reflections

Personal Reflections

Personal Reflections

Personal Reflections

Personal Reflections